SYMBOLS OF
CHINA

SYMBOLS OF CHINA

FENG JICAI

Published in English in 2009 by Compendium Publishing,
43 Frith Street, London W1D 4SA, United Kingdom.

Copyright © 2009 Yilin Press

ISBN: 978-1-849120-18-0

Text copyright © 2009 Yilin Press

Design and Art Direction by Richard Evans.

Printed and bound by Amity Printing Co., Ltd.

CONTENTS

Opposite: Chinese paper cut

PREFACE

BY ISABELLE VINSON, EDITOR-IN-CHIEF,
MUSEUM INTERNATIONAL, UNESCO

IN 53 B.C. IN CARRHAE in present-day Turkey, when the troops of the Roman general Crassus faced the Parthians for the first time, no-one could have guessed that the resounding defeat of the Republic of Rome hung on a thread. According to the legend, the defeat was due to one of the major symbols of Chinese civilisation: silk. When they unfurled their brightly coloured banners made of this precious cloth, the Cataphrachts, the heavily armoured elite of the Parthian riders, dazzled the Roman infantry and routed them. So this double effect of wonder and superior technology was the start of one of the unlikely encounters between the West and distant China, as the many tales and legends surrounding these encounters delight to tell us.

In many ways, the beautiful book on the symbols of China published by Compendium Publishing and Yilin Press is part of this same attitude. First of all, wonder. For how can we not always wonder at these cultural masterpieces, produced by individual and collective human genius, and the beauty of the Chinese landscapes? Take the Thousand Buddha Caves in Mogao, for example, with their representation of the world marching through time. Or the tomb of the first Emperor Qin Shi Huang, whose reputation in the West for greatness and splendour was such that it seemed natural to call the country he reigned over after the Qin Dynasty that he founded. Then finer technology. This was what René Étiemble analysed when he talked about *Chinese Europe* to acknowledge our debt to China and the importance of the legacy granted to this continent. And there are more symbols here. The most humanistic of them is mobile character printing, developed in China between the 7th and 13th Century by Buddhist monks in great need of copies of text. This was such a challenge to the terrible attitude of superiority of modern Europe that we felt obliged to reinvent it in about 1450 and place it in the hands of Gutenberg.

Carried by prestigious inventions, and inspired by a fascination motivated as much by science as by greed for wealth, for many years knowledge of Chinese civilisation in the West was reduced to a succession of themes and objects (Confucianism, the Silk Road, calligraphy, ceramics, bronzes, …) that were supposed to crystallise its essence. The major turn in historical regime during the 20th Century strengthened this knowledge system. By revising the value of Chinese culture for the present, it relegated its testimonies to the past. So we are justified in expecting to see an elegant and knowledgeable overview of the immense Chinese culture of the past, as the name of the publisher suggests. The book certainly has all these qualities. But those are not its greatest merits.

If we take a closer look, the title, *Symbols of China,* refers to a completely different reality from the thematic and descriptive aspects that it might suggest at first. But neither is it an extended exploration of the legendary Chinese complexity of interwoven meanings and symbols. *Symbols of China* presents a much more complex panorama of Chinese culture than indicated by the chapter headings, themselves very symbolic (*Cultural Icons, Natural Wonders, Architectural Heritage, Arts & Crafts*).

In fact some of the headings (*Ceremonies & Festival, Daily Life, Legend, Performing Arts*) stimulate our curiosity and raise questions. Since when did *Daily Life* appear in a book on Chinese symbols? And apart from what we expect from a book simplifying their history, what place should *Legends* have in Chinese culture? And are the ancestor worship ceremonies not vestiges from former social and spiritual systems with limited relevance as high-ranking symbols in contemporary China?

The diversity of subjects in this work, as well as the richness of the content, clearly shows that there has been a major revision not only by Western admirers but in the way that China regards its own culture. A key indicator of this new attitude is China's own interest in all aspects of its own heritage. In some seemingly conventional chapters, *Symbols of China* in fact sets out the main benchmarks of a new taxonomy of China's cultural and natural heritage. Nothing less.

Over the last twenty or so years, since 1987 in fact, China has had forty-two cultural and natural properties recognised by the international community. Almost all the Architectural Heritage presented here, many of the *Cultural Icons* (*including the Giant Panda*) and *Natural Wonders* are inscribed on the UNESCO World Heritage List, be they cultural, natural or mixed. Of the twelve examples of *Performing Arts* mentioned here, three of them (the Guqin and its music, Uyghur Mukam from Xinjiang and the Kun opera) are already on the Representative List of Intangible Cultural Heritage of Humanity, which began in 2001. Without denying the visibility obtained by international recognition, these listings bear witness above all to the political and social process underway in terms of cultural heritage in China. A careful study of changes in legislation on the protection of heritage in the People's Republic of China over the last half century, and a better understanding of the Chinese concept of heritage — which there is no space to present here, but which is a great help in reading this book — fine-tune and change many of our prejudices about physical conservation and transmission of values of heritage in China.

No place or period is without its material losses of cultural symbols. It is also possible to convey the social disappearance of cultural symbols from the pressure put on uses of culture. But the very principle of symbol is based on adherence to the meaning attached to the symbol. So it is not surprising to find a symbol in itself in this important book: the testimony to the place that its ancient culture holds in China today.

Professor Paul Richardson, who wrote the Introduction, has held senior management positions in international publishing companies such as Macmillan, Harper Collins and Reed Elsevier. He was also the founder and first director of the Oxford International Centre for Publishing Studies and a professor at Oxford Brookes University. He has also been a visiting professor at Beijing Normal University and the Moscow State University for Printing Arts. Professor Richardson was the first foreign research fellow at the Chinese Institute for Publishing Sciences and is on the international advisory board of China Book International. He is a frequent contributor to *China Book Business Report*, *China Publishing Today* and *China Publishers*.

INTRODUCTION

BY PROFESSOR PAUL RICHARDSON

A CHINESE PAINTING of a crane flying over a branch of plum blossom could be simply a delightful image to Western eyes, but for a Chinese viewer it may be loaded with layers of further meaning. The migratory return of the cranes is a sign of the regeneration of spring and the plum is the first tree to blossom in the year, sometimes even in time for the Chinese New Year "Spring Festival" in January or February. It is a symbol, on the one hand, of purity and of virginity, yet plum blossom also has connotations of sexual pleasure. Meanwhile the crane, on the whole a negative symbol in India and many Western mythologies, is celebrated in China as a positive symbol of longevity and wisdom. A picture of two cranes flying towards the sun might be given as a gift, conveying the wish that the recipient will enjoy success and rise high in the world.

Such a gift might be wrapped in red paper, though this would be quite inappropriate if the gift was instead one in commiseration for loss, and the paper itself might be decorated with subtle patterns, which in themselves carry further messages that can only be understood by the tutored eye.

A humble plate with a circle of dumplings on it may be more than an offering of one of China's favorite comfort foods; it also has a message of "togetherness", while eggs (fertility), fish (prosperity) and duck (fidelity) each carry their own meanings. Noodles, another Chinese staple, signify longevity and it would be appropriate to serve long noodles at the end of a meal with a friend who is about to go on a journey.

Similarly, not only foods, plants and creatures have layers of symbolism woven around them in the Chinese world view, but so too do natural wonders, such as rivers, lakes and mountains, and man-made ones such as gardens and buildings, including, of course, those huge achievements of Chinese creativity such as the Great Wall, the Grand Imperial Canal and the Forbidden City, as well as humbler artefacts and crafts, ceremonies and festivals.

While almost every aspect of the Chinese cosmos can be viewed in both its superficial and its symbolic form, there are many central cultural icons that are especially redolent in meaning and symbolic power. These may be very ancient, such as the Four Auspicious Creatures — the dragon-like loong, which symbolizes, among other things, good luck; the phoenix (fairness and good governance); the turtle (long life and wisdom); and the qi'ling, a composite beast that stands for peace and prosperity. They may also be modern, such as the five-starred flag of the People's Republic of China. Here the red stands for the revolution, the large star for the leadership of the Party, and the four smaller ones for the four participating classes in the new Chinese society.

Some of the most familiar Chinese symbols for Westerners are calligraphic Chinese characters, but for these, as with the other symbols already mentioned

Left: "Flying upon the Wind" by Chang Hsitsun
Above: loong and phoenix paper cut

above, a single connotation of "peace" or "happiness" is really a gross oversimplification, as symbols take on different and complex meanings according to their context and juxtaposition with each other.

What is beyond doubt is the enormous power and importance of symbols throughout China's long history and in everyday life in China even today.

SYMBOLS IN CONSCIOUSNESS AND HISTORY

It seems that from the dawn of history to the most primitive societies today, symbols have played an important part in human social and personal consciousness. Prehistoric scratchings on rocks, cave paintings, and carvings of stone, wood and bone suggest that people were using symbols for a variety of purposes and these early man-made symbols were not only obvious representations of the sun, the moon, people and animals, but also sometimes abstract shapes whose meaning is much harder to interpret. Certainly this is true in China, where abstract and representational signs have been found dating back to between 5,000 and 6,000 years BC. Whether these were in any way precursors of the early pictographic and, later, logographic Chinese scripts, which were developed millennia later, is open to debate, but they are examples of the pervasiveness of symbols in China from the earliest times.

There have been many modern theoretical studies of the impact of symbols in life and in dreams on the human psyche. The psychoanalyst Sigmund Freud saw them in a fairly simple and largely sexual sense, offering direct replications of the phallus and the vagina, but for his pupil and friend Carl Gustav Jung they were much more complex. Jung noted, for instance, the almost universal existence of the geometrical shapes of the mandala, found especially in Indian and Tibetan (and thence Chinese) iconography. He believed that beneath the preconscious (the mental faculties and memories that can be summoned into consciousness) and the personal unconscious (which may sometimes be jolted to the surface in dreams and recollections), there is a collective unconscious that cannot be recalled directly, but exists in symbols — sometimes described as a form of morphic resonance, a shared unconscious knowledge or memory within society.

The omnipresence and power of symbols in Chinese society might in part be explained by the strength of the collective and connected in that society (and the acceptance of the illogic of Eastern cosmology) in contradistinction to the individualistic (and rational) emphasized in modern society in the West. Interestingly this collective view of human existence long pre-dated Communism, though no doubt was strengthened by it, and is deeply embedded in the traditional ethic of Confucianism, Taoism, and other traditional Chinese world views.

Another explanation for the importance of symbols for Chinese civilization could be the length and continuity of its history. Rice and pigs were domesticated from at least 7500 BC; other animals and plants followed on soon afterwards. Silk has a history of over 5,000 years. The consumption of tea, which has a very complex symbolic role for the Chinese, has an even longer history. Given the central part these things played in people's lives over such a long period of time, it is hardly surprising that they came to take on symbolic significance beyond their immediate and mundane use.

Born in the communities of the upper Yellow River valley, Chinese civilization matured from its legendary millennia into the first historic Chinese

The Chinese drink tea for good health and simple pleasure

Empire, the Qin, in 221 BC. Thereafter it was sometimes fractured, but retained an essential continuity under successive imperial dynasties. No wonder, therefore, that its mountains, including the greatest in the world, Qomolangma (Mount Everest), were symbolically linked to the emperors. China was the Middle Kingdom, the most powerful, technologically developed and socially sophisticated society in the world until its humiliating decline and collapse in the 19th and early 20th centuries, but that could be seen as just a blip in the full sweep of its history. The empire itself was subjected to non-Han rulers, the Mongols for a hundred years from the mid-11th century and the Manchus for 250 years from the mid-17th century, but the minorities in effect submitted to Han civilization and values, and some of their own symbols were absorbed into the Chinese canon.

Many Chinese symbols are associated with the religious and ethical systems that underpinned imperial society — Confucianism, Taoism and Buddhism among others. Many early reformers of the late 19th and early 20th centuries challenged some of their precepts, and some of their practices, such as foot binding for women — itself powerfully symbolic (the deformed foot was the "three-inch golden lotus") — were outlawed, but many of the fundamental assumptions and beliefs of traditional Confucian society remained in place in post-imperial years following the 1910 revolution, despite the enormous social disorder, civil war between the Nationalists and the Communists, and the Japanese invasions.

After the Communist victory in 1949 and the establishment of the People's Republic, the old religious and social systems were more directly challenged and largely outlawed, with the process reaching its convulsive extremes during the period of the Great Cultural Revolution, 1966–1976, which witnessed a full-frontal attack by the Red Guards on all aspects of China's traditions in their actual and symbolic forms. Only the personal intervention of Prime Minister Chou Enlai prevented the destruction of the Confucius Temple in his birthplace Qufu, the very cradle of the Confucian tradition, though the damage to some of its emblematic stone pillars can still be seen.

Today only a very small proportion of China's 1.3 billion people belong overtly to formal religious organizations, but Confucian principles have been rehabilitated and, despite industrialization, urbanization, and globalization, traditional symbols and the conscious and subconscious messages they convey continue to exert a powerful influence on the way people behave in their everyday lives and on their views of the world.

CHINESE SCRIPTS

Of the "four great inventions" of Chinese history — gunpowder, the compass (itself intimately connected to the practice of fengshui), paper, and printing with moveable type — two have to do with the written word and Chinese script is immensely important in its symbolic significance. It is in a sense the glue that holds together an immense country with dozens of languages and hundreds of dialects, many mutually incomprehensible. It has the longest history of any living written language and immeasurable cultural significance.

In legend Chinese script was invented in 2650 BC by Cangjie, a scholar supposedly with four eyes and eight pupils, who served the equally legendary Yellow Emperor, drawing his inspiration from an emblematic hoof print dropped by a passing phoenix. What is certain is that in the middle and late

A column carved with bas-relief loongs in the Confucius Temple, Qufu

The walled fort city of Jiayuguan at the western terminus of the Great Wall of China

The Chinese character for "Love"

Shang dynasties (1500–1000 BC) script was etched onto turtle shells and animal bones for the purpose of divination. This "oracle bone script" was largely pictographic — it took the form of stylized drawings of real objects.

Subsequently it evolved and grew into the Greater and Lesser Seal Scripts, which became increasingly logographic, with characters representing words not images. The elegant Lesser Seal, or Xiaozhuan, is the direct parent of modern Chinese writing and survives today in calligraphy and on seals.

From about 500 BC Lishu, or the Clerkly Script, developed, simpler and more flowing than Xiaozhuan and therefore more suitable for administrative use in the running of the empire. It is the basis of the modern complex script used in Chinese Taiwan, Chinese Hong Kong and among overseas Chinese communities.

Thereafter other cursive scripts developed, and in the 1950s and 1960s the Communist government developed a simplified script as part of its great drive for literacy, which rose from single figures before 1949 to over 95 percent today. The importance of script in symbolic form is that characters can represent a variety of concepts and images in different combinations with other characters or other visual symbols.

Chinese characters have been particularly potent for Westerners, albeit often in a crude form of decoration or misspelled for tattoos for footballers, pop stars and ordinary teenagers. There may be some comfort in the fact that the most frequently searched characters on the Internet by non-Chinese people worldwide are those for love, strength, peace, happiness and friendship.

CHINESE AND WORLD SYMBOLS

Chinese characters have clearly become part of the universal language of symbols, but it is interesting to see how Chinese symbols and those in the West and other parts of the world both share meanings and also dramatically differ. It is also the case that Chinese symbols are almost always much more complex than is believed in popular Western accounts of them.

It is often said, for instance, that white is the symbol of mourning in China, but this is not strictly true, though mourning traditionally does involve the wearing of unbleached sackcloth. However, for the Chinese it is extremely unlucky to wear something white in your hair. In China white does share the universal symbolic meaning of purity, but it also symbolizes the West and the Shang Dynasty. Black, on the other hand, may represent water, the North and a salty taste. It does have connotations of death, but blackened-faced men in Chinese theater are generally honorable characters, unlike Western blackguards.

There are some symbols that seem to share universal meanings, such as the sun's association with man and the moon's with woman. The reborn phoenix is a common symbol and a positive one in many parts of the world, but the Chinese phoenix is a bird of another feather to that of the European tradition, which seems to have come down independently from Ancient Egypt via Greece to the modern Western world.

Just as the huge reservoir of Chinese characters is constantly growing to provide the language of modern life and technology, so too other symbols may also enter the canon. One curious example is Shangri-la. In 2001 the town of Zhongdian in Yunnan Province in southwest China was officially declared to be Shangri-la, the symbolic hidden valley of earthly paradise, though actually

Practising calligraphy

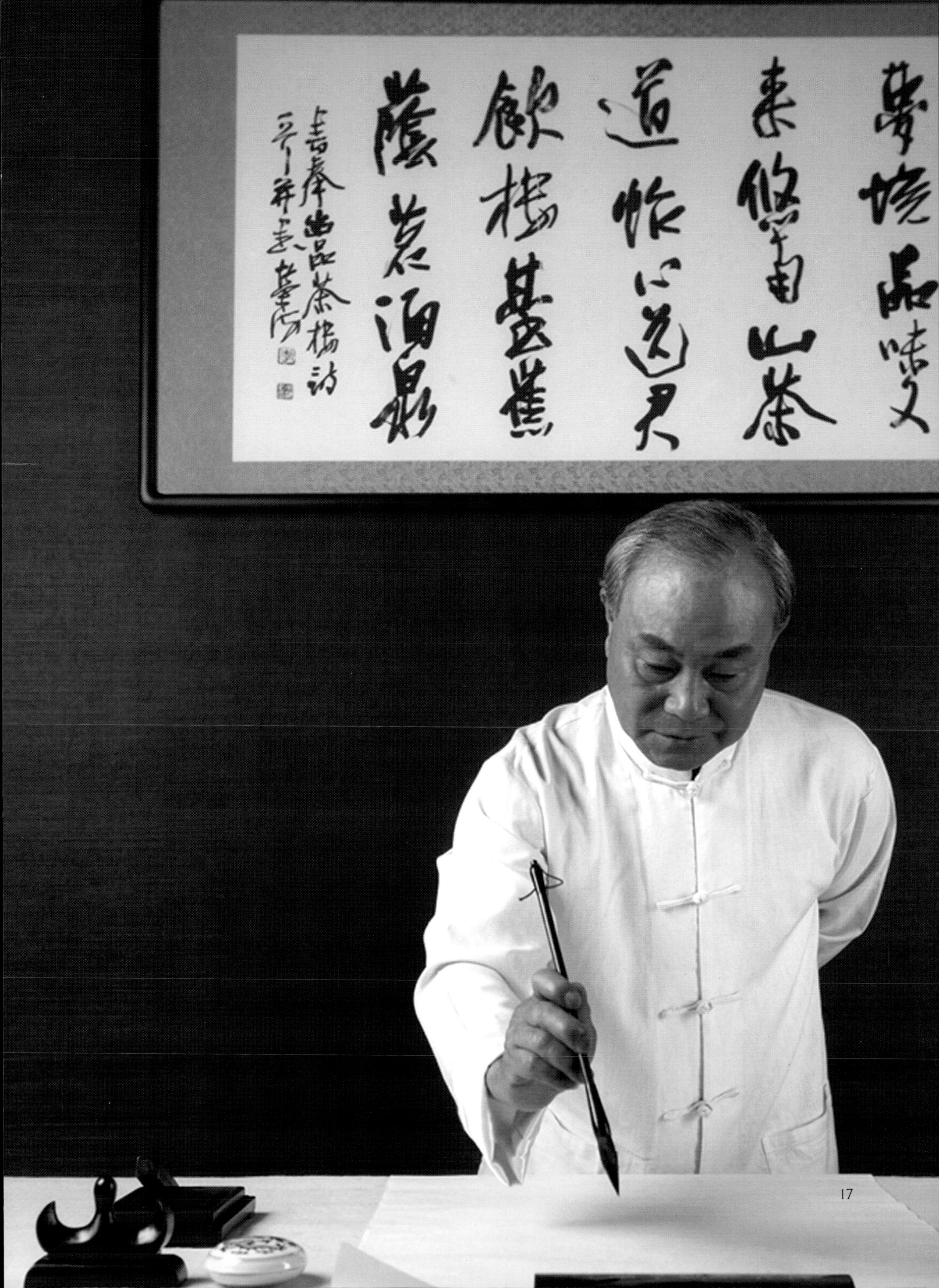

Shangri-la was a fictional construct by the British writer James Hilton in his 1933 novel *Lost Horizon*, albeit drawing on a Tibetan legend. It is, of course, no accident that the rare and luck-bringing black-necked crane breeds close to this beautiful spot to this day.

In Western society symbols and their more mundane relations, signs, are still part of everyday existence. They may still carry powerful religious or political messages. They are used extensively in company logos and overtly or subliminally in advertising and we are accustomed to their developing and changing. For instance, the positive swastika of ancient India and many other cultures including the Chinese, was debased into the emblem of the Nazis. Many Chinese symbols have also become deeply embedded in our own consciousness, for instance the interlocked semicircles of yin and yang, the balance of opposites with which many people are familiar without realizing its full significance. There is a perennial Western interest in the Chinese zodiac, though again usually in a greatly oversimplified form. Westerners are, perhaps, still more influenced by symbols than the superficially materialistic and scientific philosophies of many people would suggest. The icon has become an essential part of the language of the digital age.

However, it is arguable that Chinese symbols have a much more pervasive and complicated role, and their study reveals not just their individual meanings, but also offers an insight into divergent Chinese patterns of thought and cosmic views.

Symbols of China provides an introduction to this immensely complex and fascinating subject where, as the great collector of Chinese art Emil Preetorius wrote, "There is virtually nothing in the whole of nature, organic or inorganic, no artefact [in China which is not] imbued with symbolic meaning." The book seeks to open a door to this world, where for many Chinese symbolic language is a second tier of communication, frequently richer in nuances of meaning than everyday speech and writing.

Having absorbed its messages, the reader may recall, at the very least, that untidily discarded chopsticks at the end of a meal may presage bad luck or even death, and that a spider descending from its web may be bringing blessings from heaven.

Above: Mooncakes, traditionally eaten at the Mid-Autumn Festival
Left: A poster entitled "Happiness and Celebration with Sufficient Resources"

TIMELINE

c.60th century BC   Xiaoshan Neolithic site, Zhejiang Province

c.30th century BC–c.21st century BC
        **THREE SOVEREIGNS AND
FIVE EMPERORS PERIOD**

c.22th century BC–c.16th century BC
        XIA DYNASTY

c.16th century BC–c.11th century BC
        SHANG DYNASTY (NORTHERN CHINA)

1029 BC–256 BC	**ZHOU DYNASTY**
1029 BC–771 BC	**Western Zhou**
770 BC–256 BC	**Eastern Zhou**
770 BC–476 BC	Spring and Autumn Period
7th century BC	Xi Shi, one of the Four Beauties of China
6th century BC	Lifetime of Lao Tzu, founder of the philosophy of Taoism
551 BC–479 BC	Confucius, aka Kongzi, scholar and philosopher, author of *Lun Yu* (*Analects of Confucius*)
544 BC–496 BC	Sun Tzu, military commander, author of *The Art of War*
475 BC–221 BC	Warring States Period
340 BC–278 BC	Qu Yuan, writer, poet and patriot
259 BC–210 BC	Qin Shi Huang, first emperor of the Qin Dynasty, buried with the Terracotta Army
221 BC–207 BC	**QIN DYNASTY**
214 BC	Lingqu Canal was dug, the first canal in the world
206 BC–220 AD	**HAN DYNASTY**
206 BC–25 AD	**Western Han**
45 BC–23 AD	Wang Mang
25 AD–220 AD	**Eastern Han**
c.105 AD–219 AD	Zhang Zhongjing, one of the greatest Chinese medicine men
3rd century AD	Diaochan, one of the Four Beauties of China
c.200 AD	Zhuge Liang, one of the greatest military strategists, minister of the kingdom of Shu
220 AD–280 AD	**THREE KINGDOMS PERIOD**
220 AD–265 AD	Wei
221 AD–263 AD	Shu Han
222 AD–280 AD	Wu
265 AD–420 AD	**JIN DYNASTY**

Maple leaves in the Jiuzhaigou Valley

265 AD–317 AD	**Western Jin**
303 AD–361 AD	Wang Xizhi, the "Sage of Calligraphy"
317 AD–420 AD	**Eastern Jin**
365 AD–427 AD	Tao Qian, writer
420 AD–589 AD	**SOUTHERN AND NORTHERN DYNASTIES**
420-479	**Song** (Southern Dynasties)
479–502	**Qi** (Southern Dynasties)
502–557	**Liang** (Southern Dynasties)
557–589	**Chen** (Southern Dynasties)
386–534	**Northern Wei** (Northern Dynasties)
534–550	**Eastern Wei** (Northern Dynasties)
550–557	**Northern Qi** (Northern Dynasties)
535–556	**Western Wei** (Northern Dynasties)
557–581	**Northern Zhou** (Northern Dynasties)
581–618	**SUI DYNASTY**
602–664	Life of Xuanzang, the great Buddhist leader
618–907	**TANG DYNASTY**
701–762	Li Bai, quintessential Tang poet
719–756	Yang Yuhuan, one of the Four Beauties of China
712–770	Du Fu, late Tang poet
713–803	Construction of the Leshan Giant Buddha
603-610	Construction of the Grand Canal
755–763	An Lu Shan Rebellion
907–1125	**LIAO DYNASTY**
907-960	**THE FIVE DYNASTIES AND TEN KINGDOMS PERIOD**
907-923	**Later Liang, The Five Dynasties**
923–936	**Later Tang, The Five Dynasties**
936–947	**Later Jin, The Five Dynasties**
947–950	**Han, The Five Dynasties**
951–960	**Later Zhou, The Five Dynasties**
960–1279	**SONG DYNASTY**
960–1127	**Northern Song Dynasty**
999–1062	Bao Zheng, Northern Sony Dynasty magistrate
1033–1085	Chen Hao, Neo-Confucian sage
1033–1107	Chen Yi, Neo-Confucian sage
1037–1101	Su Shi, aka Su Dongpo, great poet
1084–1155	Li Qingzhao, great female poet and composer
1085–1145	Zhang Zeduan, great panoramic painter
1103–1142	Yue Fei, general and lyricist: composed patriotic song "River of Red"
1115–1234	Jin Dynasty
1127–1279	**Southern Song Dynasty**
1130–1200	Zhu Xi, Neo-Confucian sage
1140–1207	Xin Qiji, commander and lyricist
1162–1227	Temüjin, aka Ghengis Khan, uniter of the Mongols

The Leshan Giant Buddha

1206–1368	**YUAN DYNASTY**
1211–1215	Temüjin attacks the Jin Empire
1215	Temüjin takes Beijing
Mid-14th century	Shi Nai'an, probable writer of *The Water Margin*
1368–1644	**MING DYNASTY**
c.1505–1580	Wu Cheng'en, poet and novelist
1518	St Paul's Cathedral, Macao, built by missionaries
1616–1911	**QING DYNASTY**
1654–1722	Emperor Kangxi
1711–1799	Emperor Qianlong
1851–1864	Taiping Heavenly Kingdom
1866–1925	Sun Yat-Sen, founder of the Kuomintang, first president of the Republic of China
1881–1936	Lu Xun, writer and satirist, author of *The True Story of Ah Q*
1887–1975	Chiang Kai-shek, exiled leader
1895–1932	Liu Tianhua, musician and composer
1899	Wang Yirong discovers the first oracle bone inscriptions
1903–1987	Liang Shiqiu, renowned writer
1906–1967	Puyi, Qing Dynasty, the last Chinese emperor
1911	Footbinding forbidden
1912–1949	**REPUBLIC OF CHINA**
1949	**PEOPLE'S REPUBLIC OF CHINA**
1949	"March of the Volun teers" becomes the national anthem
1972	Jiuzhaigou Valley, Sichuan Province, officially discovered
1987	Mount Tai, the most important of the Five Sacred Mountains, becomes UNESCO site
1989	Qomolangma National Reserve established
1990	Mount Huang declared UNESCO World Heritage Site
1994	Wudang Mountain becomes UNESCO World Heritage Site
1994	Potala Palace becomes a UNESCO World Heritage Site
1996	Mount Emei, Sichuan Province, becomes a UNESCO World Heritage Site
1996	Leshan Giant Buddha becomes a UNESCO World Heritage Site
2003	Three Parallel Rivers of Yunnan Protected Areas declared a UNESCO World Heritage Site
2005	Historic Centre of Macao declared a UNESCO World Heritage Site
2008	Beijing Olympics

Mount Tai, Shangdong Province

1

CULTURAL ICONS

文化图标

书法 CALLIGRAPHY

IN A CULTURE where calligraphy has long been cherished as a major aesthetic expression, the honorary title "Sage of Calligraphy" carries enormous importance. This title, without any dispute, goes to Wang Xizhi (303–361). Wang lived in the Eastern Jin Dynasty (317–420) and held various posts in the government. While he was never a top politician, as a calligrapher he reached a social height to which few others could aspire.

Before Wang Xizhi, calligraphy was used simply for information. It was Wang who transformed calligraphy into a transcendent art form, which aims at capturing aesthetic beauty through presenting a higher order. He focused on variations of line and form and, above all, on the dynamic and rhythmic flow of energy.

The only authentic work by Wang that we can appreciate today — though some experts question it — is the *Greeting Letter After Snow*. Many experts consider it to be inferior only to *Preface to the Poems Composed at the Orchid Pavilion*. This 28-character letter is a semi-cursive script in four lines. The strokes flow gracefully and are round at the corners, expressing delight in ease.

Emperor Qianlong (1711–1799) of the Qing Dynasty was very fond of it and ranked it as the very best of his huge royal collection of precious works.

Wang Xizhi (303–361), the Sage of Calligraphy

风水 FENGSHUI

FENGSHUI seeks the fit between one's inner being and the external world. In practice, it often helps developers to choose the locations of new buildings, based on the natural landscape and the surroundings. The term "fengshui" literally refers to wind and water, which are crucial features to take into consideration when evaluating a geographic location.

The practice of fengshui, which originated in the Taoist tradition in ancient China, also held the belief that there are correlations between humans and the universe. Thus before the magnetic compass was invented, practitioners of fengshui made use of astronomy to assess the auspiciousness of a place. Buildings were designed in a way that fit the relationship of the residents and the folk understanding of the universe.

The magnetic compass, one of the four greatest inventions of ancient China, was invented arguably for the practice of fengshui, and has been in use for that ever since its inception. Other tools used in fengshui included primitive versions of the compass such as the south-pointing spoon. Later, tools specifically for use in fengshui were invented.

In the various theoretical frameworks of fengshui, it is usually stressed that a person living in a particular place should match his or her external environment, including the land, the river, and even the entire universe. It is assumed that heavenly power influences earthly lives, and that human beings should adjust themselves to the power, invisible and intangible as it may appear. For instance, following the Taoist tradition, the practitioners of fengshui study the energy flow within a person's body, and attempt to find out whether it goes with the wind or water flow in his or her surroundings. In this way, they can tell whether there is harmony between the person's inner being and the environment. This harmony can keep him or her healthy, strong and lucky.

A fengshui compass

Book of Fengshui

The use of the compass also demonstrates the Taoist tradition of fengshui. A compass indicates the magnetic polarity of the earth, while Taoism attaches great importance to the two polarities within the human body — yin and yang. In this way, the polarities of one's body are matched by the bi-polar field of the earth. The two polarities within one's body constitute the source and sink of the energy flow, which mirrors the flow of energy between the two polarities of the earth, manifested in wind or water movements.

Fengshui is practiced both in China and widely elsewhere in the world. It has attracted much attention in scholarly research as well. Many of its principles conform to those of modern ecology, and its cultural value and wisdom have gradually been recognized. Like Chinese acupuncture and herbal medicine, fengshui, as a symbol of traditional Chinese culture, is an invaluable part of Chinese history.

五星红旗 FIVE-STAR RED FLAG

THE NATIONAL FLAG of the People's Republic of China is a red rectangle emblazoned with five stars — the "Five-Star Red Flag".

The flag was officially unveiled on October 1, 1949, with the formal announcement of the founding of the People's Republic of China. At three o'clock in the afternoon of that day, Chairman Mao Zedong hoisted the first Five-Star Red Flag on a pole overlooking Tian'anmen Square.

The flag was red with a large, golden five-pointed star and four smaller five-pointed stars in the upper left corner. The red background symbolizes the spirit of the revolution, or the blood of the heroes who died during the revolution. The golden colour of the stars symbolizes the history and culture of the Chinese people and the brightness of the communist future. The five stars grouped together signify the unity of the Chinese people, with the larger star symbolizing the leadership of the Communist Party of China. The four smaller stars that surround the big star symbolize the four classes of Chinese that were considered unifiable by Mao at that historic time (from one of Mao's works: *On The People's Democratic Dictatorship*). These are the workers, peasants, petty bourgeoisie (the small business class), and the national bourgeoisie (Chinese private businessmen). The four stars represent the traditional four categories of the people in China — workers, farmers, intellectuals and businessmen.

The design of the flag was chosen out of more than 3,000 entries received in the design competition. The designer, Zeng Liansong, was at that time not an artist by trade but the secretary of the Shanghai Modern Economics News Agency. His design was finally approved by the Chinese People's Political Consultative Conference on September 27, 1949, at their first plenary session.

裹脚 FOOT BINDING

THE "THREE-INCH GOLDEN LOTUS" refers to the deformed tiny foot of a Chinese woman in pre-modern times, and the glorified description embodies a morbid concept of beauty. While obsolete today, the practice of foot binding affected countless Chinese women from the 10th to the 20th centuries. Viewed at varying times as object of art, exotic fetish, and symbol of a repressed Chinese femininity, the image of the bound foot is a disturbing artefact of suffering, an icon of a different age.

There are several versions of the story concerning the origins of foot binding. According to one version, the emperor Li Yu (reigned 961–975) ordered his concubines to wrap their feet with silk and dance on a six-foot (two-metre) high, lotus-shaped stage. Bound, their feet resembled the shape of crescent moons, and constrained their body movements to a delicate, swaying gait. The emperor was pleased, and it is said that the practice, which originated in the palace, gradually spread to the populace. By the Northern Song Dynasty (960–1279), foot binding had become common.

When a young girl was five or six years old, her mother or grandmother would bind her feet. The toes and the balls of feet were bent towards the heels, then secured and wrapped with long bandages of cloth. The pain of this practice could be imagined, and the result was that all the toes, except the big toes, would be broken. The bandages were sometimes soaked in herbal medicine, which made them contract when they dried and reinforced the binding. Women with bound feet could neither do farm work nor take an extended walk. Yet those with naturally developed feet risked rejection from marriage.

The practice of foot binding was abolished several times in history. During the Taiping Heavenly Kingdom (1851–1864), women were prohibited from binding their feet. A series of anti-binding campaigns were launched during the late Qing Dynasty (1616–1911), and a number of women unwrapped their feet as a gesture of liberation. The practice of foot binding was officially eliminated with the founding of the Republic of China in 1911.

The "three-inch golden lotus"

龙凤龟麟 FOUR AUSPICIOUS CREATURES

THE LOONG, phoenix, turtle and qi'ling are the Four Auspicious Creatures of Chinese mythology. Though even today people still cannot decide whether loong, phoenix and qilin exist or not, by no means does this uncertainty affect their high status and wide influence that are deeply rooted in the imaginary landscape of the Chinese spiritual world.

LOONG

The loong, often mis-translated as dragon, is the indisputable number one totem for the Chinese, who claim themselves as its descendants. It has a very long body of fierce appearance, a magical combination of a horse's head, a snake's neck, a deer's horns, a turtle's eyes, fish scales, a tiger's paws and a hawk's claws. Certain features may differ depending on the varieties; for example, some may have wings, but some not; some have scales, while some not.

The loong is believed to live in the deep ocean and is in charge of making clouds and rain. It can fly very high into the sky and pour down rain. Not surprisingly, in ancient times people organized holy ceremonies praying to the loong for rain when the region was plagued by drought. Part of the ritual is the loong dance, in which performers line up in a long queue holding up a loong model and mimicking the agile movements of the creature. Today the dance has become a highlight of many festive celebrations.

Unlike the ugly and evil dragon in Western legends, the Chinese loong is

The phoenix, king of all birds

Nine Loongs Wall in the Palace Museum, Beijing

awesome with dignity, symbolizes imperial authority and indicates good luck. Down through Chinese history, emperors of all dynasties proclaimed themselves to be the loong, sent down by Heaven to take charge of the secular world. The royal family monopolized the use of the loong image for decoration, for example on clothes, furniture and palaces. Any infringement upon this monopoly by anyone outside the royal family would lead to nothing but death. Today, if you visit the Palace Museum in Beijing you can still see the well-preserved Nine Loongs Wall there — it is terrific!

PHOENIX

The phoenix is a kind of divine and auspicious bird in Chinese mythology, having colourful feathers of heavenly radiance and a sweet, melodic voice. The male phoenix is called feng, and the female huang. When it dies, it consumes itself in fire and is reborn out of the ashes.

The Chinese revere the phoenix as the king of all birds, and believe that it signifies political fairness and economic prosperity. In addition, the phoenix has long been taken to symbolize the queen and other female members of the

royal family. It often appears in juxtaposition with the loong in Chinese literature and arts, such as in the saying "The loong and phoenix, good luck and great success."

TURTLE

Among the Four Auspicious Creatures, the turtle is the

only one whose existence can be verified, though the turtle in Chinese mythology possesses great supernatural power that distinguishes it from the ordinary ones that we commonly see.

The Chinese hold that some turtles can live for up to ten thousand years and are of unimaginable strength and wisdom. Some say turtles over a thousand years old can speak and think like humans. According to a popular legend, in the middle of the ocean there is a great mountain called Penglai, on which live numerous gods. Penglai rests upon the back of a divine turtle that constantly swims around and this makes it extremely hard for people to find the mountain.

Because of these legends the Chinese pay great homage to the turtle, which has become synonymous with longevity. Rich and powerful families installed turtle sculptures in their homes, often buried under the corners of their houses, to bring them long-term prosperity. And in ancient times people used turtle shells in astrology because they believed the turtle could foretell the future.

QILIN

Qilin, often shortened to lin, has the body of a deer covered with hard scales, a horn on its head, the hooves of a horse and the tail of a bull. Like the phoenix, it is seen as a propitious sign of peace and prosperity.

One story has it that some people had seen the auspicious creature qilin before the birth of Confucius. Probably because of this legend, people gradually associated qilin with talented sons. They worshipped qilin in hope of having smart and dutiful sons, the number of whom was considered a prime indicator of family prosperity in ancient China.

It is also believed that qilin can drive away evil spirits, and in the past many rich or powerful families had sculptures of qilin in their mansions. Today it is still popular to have an ornament of qilin on one's person or at home for good luck.

Qilin, a propitious sign of peace and prosperity

梅兰竹菊 "FOUR GENTLEMEN" OF CHINESE CULTURE

WHEN STUDYING Chinese culture you may come across the terms "Four Gentlemen" or "Four Noble Friends". They refer to the plum blossom, orchid, bamboo and chrysanthemum. In Confucianism "gentleman" indicates a lofty personality and upright character, of which these four plants are conceived to be the best embodiment. Their botanical features are interpreted as virtues expected of the ideal man, drawing admiration from the Chinese, who therefore often use the Four Gentlemen as the theme of paintings and poems to proclaim moral integrity.

We will now explore the virtues of the Four Gentlemen in greater detail.

PLUM BLOSSOM

If the plum blossom arrives, can spring be far behind? Because it blooms at the end of winter, the plum blossom has long been applauded as the herald of spring.

Despite the chilling weather, the plum blossom displays its beauty at a time when other flowers are still hiding from the cold. Its petals are soft and delicate, but its spirit is tough. Its pride prevents it from flowering together with others — it cannot bear that kind of degradation. Each plum blossom has five petals, which are sometimes associated with happiness, prosperity, longevity, success and peace.

In the Song Dynasty (960–1279), a famous poet named Lin Bu led a hermit's life on a hill near the West Lake in Hangzhou, Zhejiang Province, raising cranes and planting plum trees. He had no family, but took care of the plum trees as his wife and the cranes as his sons, making friends with Nature. Since then, the plum blossom is often associated with hermit life.

Native to China, the plum tree has thirty main species, which can be further divided into 300 varieties. The blossoms can be of diverse shapes and colours. The vitality of plum trees is absolutely amazing — the oldest one alive today, which grows in the County of Huangmei, Hubei Province, is estimated to be over 1,600 years old!

Plum and Blossom, by Wang Mian (1287–1359)

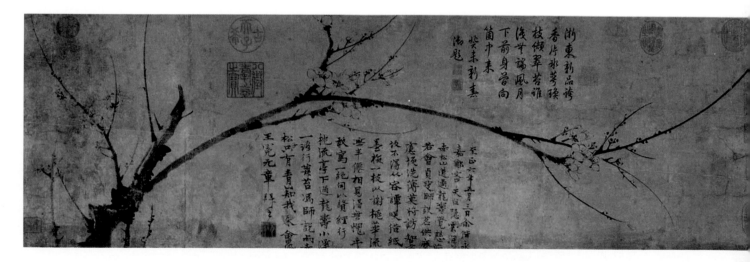

ORCHID

The orchids are a family of perennial herbs that includes as many as 20,000 varieties. Like the plum blossom, it ranks among the top ten flowers adored by the Chinese. It usually blooms in spring and the blossom commonly has three petals, which are often light green and give off a faint fragrance.

The Chinese celebrate the orchid as a symbol of moral purity and refinement, for it often grows in ravines far away from worldly noise and bustle. It is alone but not lonely, because it has achieved full realization of its beauty in its aloofness. As a "gentleman", it keeps its independence without being seduced by fame or wealth. It is quite natural that it easily arouses sympathy from people with the same attitude to life.

Since the Jin Dynasty (265–317), it has become popular to cultivate orchids in back yards or gardens. There are many monographs dedicated to orchids, and the earliest one known to us today is the *Study of Orchid in Jinmen and Zhangzhou Regions* (1233). Traditional Chinese literature abounds with odes to the orchid, in which the authors express their disdain of secular corruptions. Evidently, the orchid has always been appealing to an innermost dream of the Chinese literati — being free from vulgar minds and secular troubles.

BAMBOO

The bamboo family includes members that are one-foot dwarfs and others that are giants up to twenty feet tall. Though not blessed with dainty blossoms (bamboo commonly does not flower, but when it does, it is in danger of dying), it has won its unique place in Chinese culture with its straightness and integrity. As an evergreen plant, bamboo fully exemplifies the qualities of modesty and strength.

Bamboo has always been a pleasure for the eyes. Depending on the species, the shape of bamboo leaves varies — slim or fat, pointed or ellipsoid, banded or striped. The stems are streaked with brown, violet, or black shades and specks. Bamboo is smooth, light, hard and hollow, and these features render it a great choice for manufacturing a number of useful objects, from baskets to chairs and from fences to even houses.

More importantly, the Chinese interpret straightness as honesty, hollowness as modesty and hardness as strength. These qualities won bamboo wide respect and affection from all walks of life, and so in Chinese history, bamboo became a repeated theme in paintings and poems. Su Dongpo, a famous poet in the Song Dynasty, sighed that "For gentlemen, a meal without meat is still enjoyable, but

a garden without bamboo is unbearable."

With a little care, bamboo can grow profusely, and it would surely be great to have such a "gentleman" as your neighbour.

CHRYSANTHEMUM

Chrysanthemum, or "mum" for short, is a perennial flowering herb native to China and it has been cultivated there as an ornament for 3,000 years. It usually blooms in late autumn, delighting people's eyes and hearts with its graceful petals.

Its perseverance in the face of frost and cold has won it the reputation as a gentleman of distinguished virtue. It especially echoes to the melancholy of those who refuse to compromise with secular mediocrity and who find no place to bring their talents into full play. Many top literati in Chinese history, for instance Qu Yuan (340–278 BC) and Tao Qian (365–427), took the chrysanthemum as their spiritual friend and paid tribute to it in their works.

The chrysanthemum is also regarded as a symbol of longevity. Chinese celebrate the Double Ninth Festival, also called Chrysanthemum Festival, on the ninth day of the ninth lunar month. Traditionally it is a holiday for the elderly, who gather on this day to watch mums and climb hills or mountains.

Thanks to horticultural inventions, today we can appreciate over 3,000

Picking Chrysanthemums, by Yuan Ji (1642—1718)

37

species of mums. Depending on the species, the shape varies from daisy-like to water-lily-like, from spoon to button, from fan to hanging basket. The flower is commonly yellow, but other colours, such as white, green, pink, purple and red, are also available.

大熊猫 GIANT PANDA

THE GIANT PANDA is a national treasure in China and is therefore protected by law. The Chinese call their beloved pandas "large bear-cats". Adult pandas weigh 130–350lb (60–160kg). Their body length is 4–5ft (1.2–1.5m) with a 5-in (13-cm) tail, and they have stout, powerful limbs to grasp objects like bamboo. Their most familiar feature must be the black fur on their ears and around their eyes, muzzle, legs and shoulders, which makes the colour of their bodies close to that of their natural environment — deep forest, snow and rock. A wild giant panda's diet is almost exclusively bamboo. In zoos, they eat bamboo, sugar cane, rice gruel, a special high-fibre biscuit, carrots, apples and sweet potatoes.

Pandas, with a lifespan of 20–30 years, live in temperate-zone bamboo forests in central China, in Sichuan, Shanxi, and Gansu provinces. Among the best-recognized — but rarest — animals in the world, they are listed as endangered in the World Conservation Union's Red List of Threatened Animals. Today, an estimated 2,000 pandas are found in the wild. There are about 180 pandas in captivity in mainland China and about 20 in other parts of the world.

Much research on pandas has been conducted at the Wolong Nature Reserve in Sichuan Province. Studies there show that pandas live a solitary existence, meeting only occasionally with other pandas, except during the very brief mating season in late spring or early summer when several males come together and compete for a female. But shortly after mating, the couple splits up and the animals return to their single lives again.

The giant panda usually reaches adolescence by the age of six or seven, but maturity can occur earlier, at the age of four or five, when it is bred in captivity. They breed once a year and the pregnancy usually takes three to five months. In autumn, the mother panda will make careful preparations for her delivery. Newborn baby pandas are rather pitiful: eyes closed, furless pink skin, long tail

and unable to stand. They are extremely tiny and vulnerable when they are born, with an average weight of 3.5oz (100g). Cubs are born blind and open their eyes at about 45 days. At birth they have white skin, but within two weeks their skin turns grey where eventually the hair will be black. The mother never leaves the baby during the first weeks of its life. She holds and hugs the baby against her warm body, protecting it from harm. The cub starts to crawl at 75 to 90 days. During that period, the cub and the mother may play together: the mother rolls the cub and wrestles with it while the cub climbs on the mother's back. Cubs start to eat bamboo at five months and are weaned at six months. The cub becomes independent of its mother at about one to one and a half years of age, when it leaves its mother's territory to establish its own and fends for itself. The female panda is then able to give birth again to continue the existence of the species.

围棋　GO CHESS

GO CHESS, also known as "weiqi", is a board game for two players. With a history of more than two thousand years, it is one of the oldest games in China. In traditional Chinese culture, mastery of weiqi is vital for any cultivated person. The seemingly simple game in fact involves great stratagems and a grasp of China's rich philosophical traditions. The earliest historical descriptions of weiqi date back to 559 BC. Legend has it that the game was created by an ancient Chinese emperor to teach his son military strategies. In ancient China, mastery of weiqi was considered one of the four essential skills of the cultivated man or woman, the other three being mastery of music, calligraphy and painting. During the Tang Dynasty (618–907), weiqi became increasingly popular among both the literati and the populace, and it was introduced to Japan and Korea where it acquired great popularity.

In the game, two players alternately place black and white stones on the intersecting points of a symmetrical 19 x 19 grid. Rules are defined for occupation and capture, and the winning player is the one who secures more territory than his (or her) opponent at the end of the game, when every grid on the board has been claimed. The art of the game lies in the fluidity of territory, as established territories can become vulnerable with changes in the configuration, and claims are constantly shifting. In order to win, each player must make the most efficient use of his stones, claiming more territory while defending what is under his possession.

With its combinations of invasion and defence, action and stillness, symmetry and fluidity, the weiqi board is a microcosm of the larger universe. Unlike Western chess, with its hierarchy of pieces, all the stones of weiqi are the same, in either black or white. The two colours symbolize

the two elemental forces of the universe, yin and yang. The continuously changing configurations symbolize their dynamic interplay, representing the infinite possibilities of transformation and the varied entities of the world, changing moment by moment, stone by stone. When the stones alight on the board, they breathe life into the changing patterns, almost like atoms in the air, making up both mind and matter.

Perhaps the most remarkable thing about weiqi is its seamless marriage of simplicity and sophistication, in which an almost infinite number of possibilities are conjured up with a limited number of stones. There is no standard layout for the beginning of the game — the most important time, in which possibilities are defined — and every player lays out the first few stones in his or her own way. A testament to weiqi as an art is that supercomputers such as Deep Blue can beat world-famous chess players, but the best software for weiqi remains far below the level of an average professional player.

哈达 HADA

THE HADA, or khata, is a ceremonial silk cloth given as a gift on diverse occasions in Tibetan and Mongolian culture. It symbolizes friendship, hospitality, compassion, and goodwill. The hada was originally associated with Tibetan Buddhism, dedicated by believers to the Buddha in deep veneration.

In Tibet, the hada is usually white, like the snow on the mountains, because the white colour embodies purity and holiness. In Mongolia, the hada is blue, for it is the colour of the pure sky and the colour most loved by the Mongolian people. Hohhot, the name of the capital of Inner Mongolia Autonomous Region, in fact means "blue city".

Both Tibetans and Mongolians cherish the five-colour hada as the noblest, with the colours being blue, white, yellow, green, and red. Green stands for the river, yellow for the land, blue for the

41

sky, and white for the snow; red represents the god who guards the realms. The hada is presented at weddings, funerals, valedictions and welcoming ceremonies. It is a popular gift among friends and lovers. If one wishes to apologize to someone, one presents a hada; and if one wishes to propose, the hada serves the function of the ring.

汉字 HAN ZI [CHINESE CHARACTERS]

CHINESE CHARACTERS — Han Zi — are the basic units of the Chinese language. Each character has a single syllable and can denote a variety of meanings, and characters are combined to form words and sentences. Chinese characters are distinctive for their combination of image, sound and meaning.

The origin of Chinese characters is shrouded in myths, although archaeological evidence suggests that they have been in use for at least four thousand years. Legend has it that the characters were invented during the reign of the Yellow Emperor, around 2400 BC. While studying the different objects in the world, a man named Cangjie created a system of symbols that became the earliest characters. The historical origin of Chinese characters probably had something to do with animals such as the tortoise — the oldest Chinese inscriptions were found on oracle bones, shards of bone and tortoise shells. Excavations in Anyang (in present-day Henan Province) unearthed around 20,000 pieces. The inscriptions recorded the religious rituals of the imperial families of the Shang Dynasty (1600–1046 BC).

Chinese characters are distinctive for their composition. Many characters are pictograms, which depict the objects referred to, or ideograms, which illustrate meaning in an iconic fashion. Examples of pictograms include the characters for "sun" and "moon" — the earliest form of the "sun" character is a circle with a dot in the middle, and the the "moon" character resembles the shape of a crescent. Some compound characters are more obviously ideogrammic. For instance, when the characters for "sun" and "moon" are combined, the compound character refers to "light". When the character for "tree" is doubled, it becomes "forest". If the character for "person" is tripled, it becomes "people". Often the characters are phono-semantic, with a component denoting meaning and a component denoting sound. Upon an initial glance at the character, one can have a fairly educated guess at both the meaning and the pronunciation, even if one has never encountered it before. The combination of meaning and sound within a character also makes it easy to remember and recognize.

Chinese characters are often referred to as "square-block" characters. Each character takes up the same amount of space, and characters are written with a fixed order of strokes. A list of names is generally organized according to the number of strokes in the first character of each name, instead of the alphabetical order produced by pinyin. At the opening ceremony of the Beijing Olympics, the country teams were sequenced according to the number of strokes in the first character of the country's name in Chinese.

Through the long history of the Chinese language, a number of different scripts, or writing styles, have gradually emerged. The ancient Seal Script, which originated during the Spring and Autumn Period (770–476 BC), has been preserved thanks to the first emperor of the Qin Dynasty, Qin Shi Huang, who

The Chinese character for "wood" resembles the shape of a tree, and when it is doubled, it means "forest".

The Chinese character for "person" looks like a walker, and when it is tripled, it means "people".

Right: Huabiao at Tian'anmen Square in Beijing

standardized the script. The Seal Script is still widely used today in calligraphy. Other well-known scripts include the Clerkly Script, the regular script, and the semi-cursive script. Advanced word-processing software today can easily switch from one script to another, in much the same way that it can change the typeface of an English text.

华表　HUABIAO PILLARS

WHEN YOU VISIT old palaces, imperial tombs or altars in China, you may see one or more pairs of marble pillars at the entrances called "huabiao"(pronounced "hwa-bee-ow") pillars.

Historians still have doubts as to when and why people created the huabiao. One story has it that their origin can be traced back 4,000 years ago. People at that time built tall wooden pillars on the main roads similar in function to our contemporary street and traffic signs. In addition, passers-by could leave their views on the pillars, which therefore served the same function as contemporary graffiti and internet bulletin boards. Some Chinese minorities such as the Mongolians still have these traditional pillars.

According to another version, the huabiao came from an apparatus named "biao". The biao was created as early as the Spring and Autumn Period (770–476 BC) for architectural use, for instance for determining the positions of buildings. For the preservation of the biao in long-term, big-scale construction projects, workers built it of stone rather than wood. The biao eventually changed into the huabiao, an ornament for grand architecture.

A pair of huabiaos usually has four main parts — a square base with a lotus and wave design, a column engraved with intertwined loongs and clouds, a tray supported by the pillar, and a squatting beast called a "hou" on top. The hou, a legendary auspicious animal, looks like a combination of a horse, a loong and a pterosaur. As one of the loong's nine sons, it has been worshipped by the Chinese since antiquity.

The most famous pairs of huabiaos are located at Tian'anmen Square in Beijing, built there during the Ming Dynasty in the 15th century. The pair outside the Tian'anmen gate face south, while the other pair inside the gate face north. According to folk tales, they were built not only for decoration but also as reminders for the emperor. Upon his return from an outing, the hous outside the gate conveyed the message "Stop hanging out! Return to the palace to work!" The hous inside the gate surveilled the emperor's life inside the Forbidden City. They would tell him "Please stop indulging in a sumptuous life! Go out to see the hard lives of your people!" Modern variations of huabiao are used for purely ornamental purposes. In the opening ceremony of the 2008 Beijing Olympic Games, many pairs of huabiaos were featured in the performance as a symbol of the aesthetics in traditional Chinese architecture.

易经 *I-CHING*

THE *I-CHING*, also known as *The Book of Changes*, is a classical text of Chinese cosmology. Legend has it that the I-Ching can be traced back five thousand years, to the time of mythical rulers Fu Xi and Yu. Archeological evidence of oracle bones and inscriptions date back to the Shang Dynasty (1700–1046 BC) and the Zhou Dynasty (1029–256 BC). An ancient annotated manuscript of the *I-Ching* found at the Mawangdui site near Changsha in Hunan Province is arguably attributed to Confucius.

The cosmology of the *I-Ching* reveals a universe of infinite possibilities, decipherable through simple permutations of values in a binary system, as randomly or semi-randomly generated by throws of yarrow stalks or coins. The first character of the title, "I" (read as YEE), has a twofold meaning: simplicity and transformation. The second character, "Ching", denotes that which is principled and patterned. Combined, the name thus points to a world in which order is embedded in chaos, decipherable through a text which describes the patterns of change, or the nature of transformations.

At the centre of the *I-Ching* lies the 64 hexagrams, each a combination of two trigrams, also known as "gua". Each trigram contains three lines; a broken line indicates "yin", whereas a straight line indicates its opposite, "yang". The possible combinations of three broken and straight lines give a total of eight unique trigrams. Each trigram has a name and interpretation. Three straight lines, for instance, represent the heavens, whereas three broken lines represent the earth. The trigrams can refer to natural elements such as fire, thunder, wind, and water; they can also be interpreted to reveal the course of things, from that which is stagnant to conflict and motion. Traditionally, yarrow sticks or coins are used to help generate the hexagrams, which are then interpreted in the context of the query.

The *I-Ching* has profoundly influenced both Confucian and Taoist thought, and is associated with a much larger tradition which includes practices of healing such as taiji. As one of the oldest and most profound canon of Chinese civilization, it is a must book for intellectuals and exerts a great book for intellectuals and exerts a great influence on other Asian countries. It enables us to see how the ancients perceived the world millenia ago, and remains a living art with invaluable potentials.

A copy of the I-Ching printed in the Qing Dynasty (1616–1911)

龙袍 IMPERIAL LOONG ROBE

THE CHINESE LOONG is a long, scaled, snake-like mythical creature. Unlike the European dragon, which is usually portrayed as evil, it is a symbol of auspicious fortune and imperial power. The first legendary Chinese emperor, Huang Di, is said to have been immortalized into a loong and ascended to heaven. Regarding Huang Di as their ancestor, the Chinese people refer themselves as "the descendants of the loong".

Since as early as the Zhou Dynasty (1029–256 BC), the loong has been a symbol of the king or emperor. From the late Song Dynasty (960–1279), emperors have worn luxurious robes decorated with loong patterns. During the Qing Dynasty (161–1911), the imperial robe for the emperor, which was usually bright yellow, was called "the loong robe".

The basic pattern of the imperial robe is simple. It is a long robe, usually down to the knees, with long sleeves and a circular opening for the neck. The simplicity of the pattern is offset by the intricacy and richness of the fabric and decoration. There is usually a large loong in the centre of the garment with two smaller loongs on the sleeves, two on the waist and one hidden on the inner side of the robe. There are twelve motifs altogether — loong, axe head pattern, fu pattern, the sun, the moon, the star constellation, mountain, fire, grain, the auspicious bird, cup, and water reeds on the robe, which became the most famous and representative imperial robe throughout history. The robe was mainly made of silk, with colourful patterns embroidered on it. There are a total of nine golden loongs embroidered on the robe. Observed from either the front or the back, one can see five loongs at a glance, since in Chinese culture the figures nine and five represent the dignity of the throne.

On the front of the bright yellow robe, hovering above the foaming water, is a pair of cups which symbolize filial piety. There are also water reeds, which symbolize cleanness and purity. Above waist level, at either side of the loong, are an axe head pattern — symbolizing the emperor's power over difficulties, life and death, war and famine — and a fu pattern symbolizing distinction. Above the loong, a star constellation comprised of three circles can

Fu pattern on the robe

be seen. Curling over the shoulders of the robe at either side,are the red sun and white moon. The sun, the moon and the constellation symbolize the light and wisdom of the emperor shining on the world. Mountains, symbolizing stability; loongs, symbolizing adaptability to changes; auspicious bird, denoting elegance and beauty; grain, symbolizing education; and fire, symbolizing light adorn the back. The twelve motifs are used exclusively for the emperor.

According to the imperial rituals, the imperial robe for the emperor was an auspicious garment for celebrations and ceremonies. It was in every respect the highest grade of imperial attire, and it represented supreme authority and power in Chinese history.

玉 JADE

JADE IS A UNIQUE MINERAL and is endowed with very special significance. Comparable with the way gold and diamonds are regarded in the West, jade is prized in China as being even nobler. It symbolizes imperial power, authority, nobility, virtue, pureness and luck. Considered more valuable than gold or silver in Chinese culture, jade became a favourite material for many personal items as well as ceremonial articles such as plates and gravestones.

Throughout China's long history, jade has always been associated with imperial power. The highest quality Hetian jade is China's "National Stone". Since the Qin Dynasty (221–207 BC), jade has been the exclusive material for the imperial seal. Even in Chinese mythology, the widely acknowledged ruler of both heaven and earth is called the "Jade Emperor".

A piece of loong-shaped jade jewellery

Besides the imperial authority, jade was metaphorically equated with human virtues, because of its hardness, durability, and purity. An ancient Chinese saying goes "Gentlemen should be like jade." Confucius also declared that jade had eleven virtues, such as humanity, righteousness and politeness, and therefore it became the ideal material for the personal ornaments of Chinese intellectuals, carved into paint-brush holders, paperweights, and seals. As a symbol of power, purity, perfection, and pricelessness, jade was inlaid into the Olympic medals in 2008 Beijing Olympic Games with the approval of the International Olympic Committee.

This horn-shaped jade cup is an especially exquisite vessel. When discovered in the tomb of the emperor of the Southern Yue (203–111 BC), this utensil amazed the world with its beauty and the technical skill that went into its manufacture. The cup is carved out of Hetian jade and mahogany. The thin cup wall appears semi-transparent in the sunshine, showing the superb polishing skills of its maker. It is shaped like a conch or rhinoceros horn, and the long, winding rope-shaped tail stretching out from the bottom twists around the surface of the lower body. The ornamentation of the body with three-layer painted patterns shows the originality and highlights the three-dimensional effect.

JADE CLOTHES SEWN WITH GOLD THREAD

Jade Clothes Sewn with Gold Thread look just like suits of armour. Actually, they were funeral suits for the imperial family. Dressing the dead in jade clothes was a custom that first appeared in the Warring States Period (475–221 BC) and prevailed in the Han Dynasty (206 BC– 220 AD).

As a symbol of status, jade suits, which were tailored to the client's body shape, were used as garments for the deceased emperors and the nobility of the Han Dynasty. The emperor wore garments sewn with gold thread, while princes and princesses wore silver-threaded suits; other officials and nobles wore copper-threaded garments (the latter two were called Jade Clothes Sewn with Silver Thread and Jade Clothes Sewn with Copper Thread respectively).

Since people of the Han Dynasty believed jade had absorbed the excellence of mountains, it was used to preserve dead bodies for the afterlife and jade suits were therefore among the most important jade articles. To date, over 20 jade suits have been discovered in China, including the Jade Clothes Sewn with Gold Thread for Liu Sheng, Prince Zhongshan of the Han Dynasty — the earliest and finest specimen. Early on in the Han Dynasty, Jade Clothes Sewn with Gold Thread were allowed for all nobility besides emperors. When this jade suit first came to light, it had fallen apart. The pieces were later carefully reassembled and the suit was restored to its original condition by experts.

The jade garment, 6ft (1.88m) long, was unearthed in 1968 in the Tomb of Prince Zhongshan in Mancheng County, Hebei Province, northern China. Composed of six parts — the hood, coat, sleeves, gloves, trousers and shoes, with a total 2,498 jade pieces and 1,100 grams of gold thread — the jade suit includes eye covers, nose stoppers and covers for the genitalss. The whole suit is rimmed with red thread, with an iron rim on the trouser legs for fixation. The face cover is carved with holes in the shape of eyes, a nose and a mouth. The suit is broader in the chest and back and bulges at the hips, to make it close-fitting.

The jade suit was delicately designed with carefully aligned and harmoniously coloured jade slices that reflect the exceptional techniques of the craftsmen. The jade suit is now housed in the Antique Research Centre of Hebei Province.

It can be imagined that making such a jade garment more than 2,000 years ago was far from an easy task. Raw materials had to be transported from jade mountains far away and then processed into thousands of pieces of various sizes. Every piece had to be polished and small holes were drilled into it — techniques that required amazing workmanship. The size and shape of each piece was strictly designed as part of the overall artwork and special gold thread was needed to sew the jade pieces together. Massive amounts of manpower and resources were needed to produce a piece of jade clothing. The value of such garments at the time was roughly equal to the properties of 100 middle-class families. However, items like the Jade Clothes Sewn with Gold Thread did not help emperors achieve immortality; instead, they attracted many tomb raiders. During the Three Kingdoms Period (220–280), this funeral practice was abolished because of its extravagance.

Jade deer

Jade phoenix

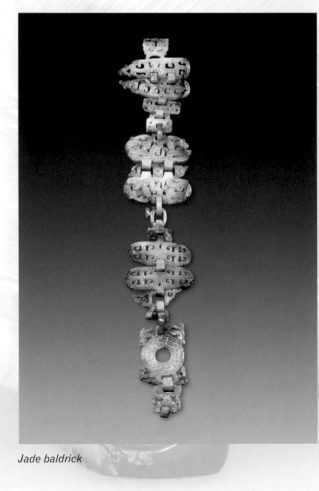

Jade baldrick

Jade plaques

Jade loong

满汉全席 MANCHU-HAN IMPERIAL FEAST

THE MANCHU-HAN IMPERIAL FEAST, or Feast of Complete Manchu-Han Courses, is probably the grandest of Chinese culinary events. It was reserved for the imperial family and high-ranking officials, and was an extravagant event that lasted three days and included six banquets and 108 exquisite dishes.

The feast originated during the Qing Dynasty (1616–1911), when it was served on the occasion of important festivals and celebrations. The Manchus were originally a tribal people of northern China. Allegedly, the Manchu emperor attempted to appease his Han subjects by entertaining Han and Manchu officials together, giving them equal honour in court and encouraging exchanges. In light of the times, when Han officials were routinely slighted in the Manchu court, this was an extraordinary diplomatic gesture.

The veritable feast featured an amazing assortment of concoctions and at least 108 courses. Only the choicest raw materials were used, and the menu featured rare and exorbitant items such as bear paws and rhinoceros tails. Today, many of the ingredients are no longer available, as many of the animals are now endangered.

At the feast, much importance was given to tableware and etiquette. The utensils and chopsticks were made of gold, silver, jade, ivory and fine china, decorated with elaborate patterns. At such a royal occasion, the guests were required to adhere to strict procedures and table manners while savouring the courses. While they dined, traditional Chinese music and dancing were performed for their entertainment.

Though the complete menu of this grand feast has been lost, the Manchu-Han Imperial Feast maintains its presence in Chinese cuisine. Select courses are still served during important banquets. The term "Manchu-Han Imperial Feast" itself has been adopted into the popular idiom. However, if someone tells you he had such a feast, do not believe that he was really treated like an emperor with 108 courses; he simply means that he enjoyed a great, delicious meal.

鸳鸯 MANDARIN DUCKS

THE MANDARIN DUCK (*Aix galericulata*) is a beautiful bird native to China. In ancient times, people believed that the bird always travelled in pairs, and thus it came to symbolize love and fidelity. Today, "mandarin ducks" is used as a metaphor for loving couples, and newlyweds often decorate their quilt-covers and bedroom with motifs of this bird.

The male mandarin is among the most colourful and exquisite of waterfowl, with an orange and green crest, a red bill, and a broad white stripe around its eyes. Two white stripes adorn its lavender breast. The female is less flamboyant; it is brown in colour, with a white stripe around the eyes and a small white stripe on each flank.

The mandarin duck nests in trees close to the water and feeds primarily on plants, seeds and insects. It is now a protected species.

义勇军进行曲 MARCH OF THE VOLUNTEERS

"MARCH OF THE VOLUNTEERS" is the national anthem of the People's Republic of China. It first appeared as a theme song in the patriotic film *Heroes in an Era of Turbulence* (1935). The lyrics were written by Tian Han, and the music composed by Nie Er, who was at the time only 23 years old.

The film *Heroes in an Era of Turbulence* tells the story of the poet Xin Baihua, who became a soldier to defend his country against the Japanese invasion. Played both at the beginning and the end, "March of the Volunteers" affirmed the determination and relentless spirit of the protagonist and the Chinese people. With the release of the film, the song, with its rousing lyrics and patriotic sentiment, captured audiences throughout China and became a hit. The lyrics are as follows:

Arise! All who refuse to be slaves!
With our flesh and our blood
We shall forge a new Great Wall!
The Chinese nation is facing its greatest peril,
and every man is roaring with his last cry.
Arise! Arise! Arise!
Our millions of hearts beating as one nation,
We brave the enemy fire, marching on!
We brave the enemy fire, marching on!
Marching on! Marching on! On!

In September 1949, "March of the Volunteers" was declared the provisional national anthem of the People's Republic of China. In 1982, the 5th National People's Congress voted to return the national anthem to these original lyrics (following the adoption of new lyrics in 1978), a decision that was officially ratified through a constitutional amendment in 2004.

如意 RUYI

THE RUYI IS AN ORNAMENT symbolizing good fortune, and its name means "as one wishes". It features a long, S-shaped handle and a frontal lobe which is in the shape of auspicious clouds or lingzhi, reishi mushrooms which symbolize longevity.

The ruyi can be made from many different materials, including jade, gold, silver, ivory and crystal, and occasionally even iron and bamboo. It is sometimes decorated with precious jewels depicting floral patterns.

The ruyi was probably introduced into China from India as a ceremonial sceptre used by Buddhist monks and it became popular during the Jin Dynasty (265–420). Nobles and government officials held ruyi during formal social occasions, using it to show respect for others. In this regard, the ruyi served a similar function to that of a top hat in the West.

Though its use and popularity varied in later dynasties, the ruyi gradually became an emblem of wealth and power. The craftsmanship of the ruyi makers reached its peak during the Qing Dynasty (1616–1911). Court officials submitted exquisitely made ruyi to the emperor as tributes on important festival days and at imperial ceremonies. In turn, the emperor also bestowed ruyi upon his officials. Today, the Palace Museum in Beijing holds nearly 3,000 pieces of ruyi of all sizes and designs.

The ruyi is not only reserved for the privileged, but is used among the populace as well. It is often given as a gift, and the image of the ruyi is a common decoration on buildings and furniture. In paintings, the god of wealth often holds a ruyi in his hand.

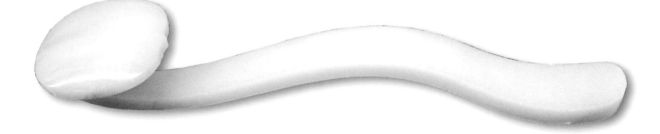

丝绸之路 SILK ROAD

THE SILK ROAD, or Silk Route, was an extensive network of trade routes across the Asian continent that connected Asia with the Mediterranean world, extending to North Africa and Europe. The first person to use the name was the German geographer Ferdinand von Richthofen, in 1877, to mark the extensive Chinese silk trade, the main reason for which the road was created. Such a name indicates the prime position of silk in ancient times. In ancient times, every Roman lady was proud to have a silk gown. Therefore, the market price for a pound of silk rose to as high as 21 ounces (600g) of gold, which resulted in the loss of gold from the Roman Empire. Because of this, the Romans imposed a ban on the importation of silk. Besides these Roman ladies, Cleopatra, the Queen of Egypt, was also said to be a big fan of silk. There are official accounts of the silk dress she wore when she met with foreign ambassadors.

Japan

Korea

China

India

Different
routes of
Silk Road

The Silk Road, over 5,000 miles (8,000km) long, was actually not only for silk but also for many other products. It enabled people to transport goods, especially luxuries such as silk, satins, musk, rubies, diamonds, pearls and herbs. Moreover, it was an important path for the spread of knowledge, ideas, and cultures — as well as diseases. It linked different parts of the world together, and significantly stimulated the development of the civilizations along the route. Some people believe that it was the Silk Road that helped to lay the foundations for the modern world. During the 1st century, Buddhism began to be introduced to China with a semi-legendary account by an emissary who travelled to the West along the Silk Road at the request of a Chinese emperor. The period of the High Middle Ages in Europe and East Asia saw major technological advances, including the diffusion through the Silk Road of gunpowder, the astrolabe, the compass and the precursor to movable-type printing. Around the Yuan Dynasty (1206–1368), the Venetian explorer Marco Polo also travelled along the Silk Road to China. He was one of the first Europeans to visit China, and his tales, documented in *Il Milione* (known in English as *The Travels of Marco Polo*), opened Western eyes to a prosperous and mysterious ancient country — China. He was not the first to bring back stories, but his account was one of the most widely read. The world benefited a lot from the Silk Road, and so did China, which was regarded as one of the most prosperous nations in the world by Adam Smith in the 18th century. The American scholar Edward Schafer wrote in his book *The Golden Peaches of Samarkand: A Study of T'Ang Exotics* that in 7th-century China, people from court officials to ordinary civilians desired all kinds of luxuries and treasures imported via the Silk Road.

The Silk Road includes both the continental route and the sea route; however, the former route is better known. China, an ancient commercial centre of the world, played a major role in the prosperity of the routes. In around 114 BC, during the Han Dynasty, the Asian part of the route expanded, largely because of the explorations of a court official named Zhang Qian. In the late Middle Ages, transcontinental trade via the Silk Road declined as sea trade increased. The routes of the Silk Road varied with geographical, political and religious changes as time passed, but according to some historical documents, the continental part of the Silk Road generally consists of the northern and the southern parts. The northern part, which is the narrowly defined and original Silk Road, starts at Chang'an (now called Xi'an), once the capital of ancient China, and extends roughly northwestward in three directions. The southern route is mainly a single route, beginning in the Sichuan Basin in China and finally arriving in Italy, Anatolia, or North Africa. The sea routes appeared later, during the Eastern Han Dynasty (25–220 AD), and led from the mouth of the Red River, through Southeast Asia and on to the Persian Gulf before ending in Roman ports.

The spirit of the Silk Road and the will to enhance exchange between the East and West, as well as the huge benefits that followed, have affected much of the history of the world during the last three millennia, and the influence may well continue into the future.

太极八卦 SUPREME ULTIMATE OF THE EIGHT TRIAGRAMS

TAIJI, THE SUPREME ULTIMATE, is a description of the state of undifferentiated absolute and of infinite potentiality in the beginning of the universe. The movement and tranquility of taiji give birth to yin and yang, two opposite yet complementary forces within a whole. Yin and yang generate Bagua, the Eight Trigrams (namely Qian, Xun, Kan, Gen, Kun, Zhen, Li and Dui), which correspond respectively to the eight main forces in the natural world, namely, heaven, wind, water, mountain, earth, thunder, fire and marsh.

In the diagram of taiji, a curved line separates the circle into two halves, one white and the other black. The white represents yang and the black yin. There is a black dot in the white part and a white dot in the black part, signifying that there is yin in yang and there is yang in yin. It visually indicates that everything in the universe involves the two opposite but complementary forces of yin and yang. The symbols on the national flag of South Korea are a testimony to taiji's immense influence in Asia.

Everything has both yin and yang aspects, which interrelate and constantly interact, never existing in absolute tranquility. In the Eight Trigrams, the solid bar "—"represents yang and the broken bar "– –" represents yin. Each trigram contains three bars. For example, the Qian trigram of heaven contains three solid bars and the Kun trigram of earth contains three broken bars. The trigrams represent clockwise different stages in the cycle of increase and decrease of yin and yang.

The Supreme Ultimate and the Eight Trigrams have been widely applied to various fields in Chinese culture such as fortune telling and fengshui (literally wind-water). The Supreme Ultimate and the Eight Trigrams emphasize the balance of yin and yang. It is believed that if you want to be a lucky person, you have to move to an environment to bring yin and yang into harmony. Fortunetellers can tell you how to achieve that by observing and analyzing the Eight Trigrams.

The fengshui in the construction of houses and cemeteries is another important use of the Supreme Ultimate and the Eight Trigrams. When ancient Chinese were going to build their houses or cemeteries, the first thing they did was to have the places of construction closely examined. Zhu Yuanzhang, the founder of the Ming Dynasty (1368–1644), built his mausoleum in the Purple Mountain in Nanjing after ordering fortunetellers to explore the fenshui of the mountain thoroughly.

The Supreme Ultimate and the Eight Trigrams also embody the harmony between human and nature, an important notion in Chinese culture. Chinese people believe that the perfect state of life is the integration of human with nature.

茶 TEA

OF THE THREE most popular beverages in the world, tea, coffee and cola, tea is distinctly Chinese. Cina is the cradle of tea, and over a quarter of the tea consumed in the world every year is produced there. Although it is not currently the biggest tea-exporting country, China maintains the longest tradition of growing, preparing and enjoying the beverage.

Chinese teas are loosely classified according to the methods by which they are processed. Apart from the non-fermented green tea and the thoroughly fermented black tea, widely consumed Chinese teas include the wulong (a kind of half-fermented tea), the pu'er (a compressed, over-fermented tea), the huacha (a scented tea comprised of tea leaves blended and dried with fresh flower buds such as jasmine), and the liangcha (an herbal blend with dried medicinal plants such as sweet-smelling honeysuckle). Teas often derive their names from their places of origin — "Lushan Yunwu", for example, means "Cloud and Mist of Lushan Mountain"); sometimes the names are also derived from the shapes of tea leaves — "Queshe" tea, for instance, means "Bird's Tongue" tea.

Traditionally, serving and drinking tea is an art, involving elaborate procedures and formalities, as in the practice of "Gongfu Tea". Evolved among the literary circles of the Tang (618–907) and Song (960–1279) dynasties, it acquired wide popularity during the Qing Dynasty (1616–1911) in the southern provinces of Guangdong and Fujian. To brew gongfu tea, one must first rinse the tea set with pristine spring water. After the tea leaves (usually of the wulong variety) are dropped into the teapot and boiling water is poured in, a series of formalities follow. The tea is then poured into elegant teacups in a graceful manner. To drink, one takes a whiff of the tea, contemplating its subtle fragrance, and then sips it, holding a small sip in the mouth and savouring the taste fully before swallowing.

The ancient Chinese regarded the best tea buds as those that carried only one or two newly grown leaves, to be picked in the mountains just around the time of the Grain Rains (the 6th of the 24 Chinese Solar Terms in the Chinese calendar, which falls approximately on the 20th of April in the Gregorian calendar). To obtain the best flavour, the ancients drew water from pure water sources such as natural springs. For instance, it is said that for taste, "West Lake's Loong Well", a green tea grown by Hangzhou's West Lake is to be brewed only with the water of "Tiger-

Running Spring" by the West Lake.

Since the middle of the Ming Dynasty (1368–1644), purple clay teaware, which is made from the purple clay produced in Yixing, Jiangsu Province, has become widely popular among connoisseurs of tea. The incrustations on the inner walls of the teapots and teacups lend a special fragrance to the tea itself, enriching the flavour of the brew.

The term "chadao" (literally "the way of tea") captures the deep cultural meanings associated with the Chinese tea ceremony. The scrupulousness in the preparation and drinking of tea scrapes only the surface; on a deeper level, chadao, informed by the Buddhist, Confucian and Taoist traditions, speaks to a uniquely Chinese attitude towards life, expressing an aspiration for aesthetic perfection and an appreciation for inner cultivation.

While the Chinese chadao originated among the refined literati in times of old, drinking tea remains ever popular. Tea was and still is the most popular non-alcoholic beverage enjoyed by ordinary Chinese people on a day-to-day basis. It is perhaps with this observation that Liang Shiqiu (1903–1987), a renowned Chinese writer, would remark, "How can a person be a Chinese if he does not drink tea?"

Making tea at a banquet

天干地支 TIANGAN AND DIZHI—THE TRADITIONAL CHINESE CALENDAR AGENDA

TIANGAN AND DIZHI refer to a set of characters that are traditionally used to record time in China. As you can see from Diagram 1, there are ten Tiangan (heavenly stems) and twelve Dizhi (earthly roots). Tiangan is also shortened as gan (stem), and Dizhi, as zhi (root). One gan and one zhi together make a gan-zhi unit, which can designate one year, one month, one day or a specific hour. This system of gan-zhi plays a significant role in Chinese culture, especially in chronology and astronomy.

This system came into being in 2697 BC when the ancestor of the Chinese, the Yellow Emperor, established his country, but an earlier origin story has it that scholars learned it from the patterns on a loong's body and on a tortoise's shell. These two patterns are called "hetu" (Picture from the River) and "luoshu" (Book from Lu River), and they are closely associated with *the I-Ching*.

The ten Tian'gan follow a fixed order, as do the twelve Dizhi. They are paired in their respective order and form a cycle of sixty gan-zhi units. In the Chinese lunar calendar, a year consists of twelve months, and each Dizhi corresponds to one month. A day is divided into twelve periods, also reckoned in terms of twelve Dizhi. So any specific time can be recorded with four gan-zhi units (the first unit designating the year, the second the month, the third the day, and the last the time period).

The stems are still widely used nowadays in counting systems. This use is similar to the way the alphabet is used in English, for instance, in legal documents or contracts where, instead of names, terms such as Party A and Party B are used.

According to the Chinese astrology, the twelve Dizhi are also associated with twelve animals — respectively the rat, bull, tiger, rabbit, loong (Chinese dragon), snake, horse, ram, monkey, rooster, dog and pig. Don't be surprised when you hear the Chinese say 2010 is the year of tiger.

干 支 表

1 甲子	2 乙丑	3 丙寅	4 丁卯	5 戊辰	6 己巳	7 庚午	8 辛未	9 壬申	10 癸酉
11 甲戌	12 乙亥	13 丙子	14 丁丑	15 戊寅	16 己卯	17 庚辰	18 辛巳	19 壬午	20 癸未
21 甲申	22 乙酉	23 丙戌	24 丁亥	25 戊子	26 己丑	27 庚寅	28 辛卯	29 壬辰	30 癸巳
31 甲午	32 乙未	33 丙申	34 丁酉	35 戊戌	36 己亥	37 庚子	38 辛丑	39 壬寅	40 癸卯
41 甲辰	42 乙巳	43 丙午	44 丁未	45 戊申	46 己酉	47 庚戌	48 辛亥	49 壬子	50 癸丑
51 甲寅	52 乙卯	53 丙辰	54 丁巳	55 戊午	56 己未	57 庚申	58 辛酉	59 壬戌	60 癸亥

TWELVE DIZHI

子	丑	寅	卯	辰	巳
午	未	申	酉	戌	亥

DIZHI AND ITS CORRELATED PAIRS

Earthly Roots	Lunar Months	Time Periods	Chinese Zodiac
子 (zi)	Month 11	11pm to 1am (midnight)	Rat
丑 (chou)	Month 12	1am to 3am	Ox
寅 (yin)	Month 1	3am to 5am	Tiger
卯 (mao)	Month 2	5am to 7am	Rabbit
辰 (chen)	Month 3	7am to 9 am	Loong
巳 (si)	Month 4	9am to 11am	Snake
午 (wu)	Month 5	11am to 1pm (noon)	Horse
未 (wei)	Month 6	1pm to 3pm	Ram
申 (shen)	Month 7	3pm to 5pm	Monkey
酉 (you)	Month 8	5pm to 7pm	Rooster
戌 (xu)	Month 9	7pm to 9pm	Dog
亥 (hai)	Month 10	9pm to 11pm	Pig

TEN TIANGAN

甲	乙	丙	丁	戊	己	庚	辛	壬	癸

A cycle of sixty gan-zhi units

中医中药 TRADITIONAL CHINESE MEDICINE

ANCIENT CHINESE PEOPLE used traditional Chinese medicine (TCM) as early as the Neolithic period. In 2001, archaeologists discovered the Xiaoshan Neolithic site in Xiaoshan, Zhejiang Province, where an earthen vessel that had been used to brew herbal medicine was found. This is the earliest record of TCM in Chinese history. Legend goes that Shennong, the tribal leader also known as the Yan Emperor, was the first Chinese who spread knowledge of using plants to treat illness. Medical professors use a book named after this legendary figure as teaching materials and this reference book, *Shennong's Herbal Classic*, is considered the first pharmacopoeia of TCM in the world. But in fact, this classical dictionary was compiled around the 2nd century BC.

As a cultural symbol with a long history, TCM now suffers from confusion and criticism. Here we would like to provide some clarifications about TCM. First, what can be considered as medicine in the TCM system is not limited to herbs only. It is known that ancient Chinese considered certain plant species to be of medical values and developed methods to extract the healing power from different parts of a plant. Besides herbal medicines,

however, it is also a common practice among doctors of TCM to use animal organs and blood products, either fresh or cured, to produce a multi-element formula. As well as these ingredients, non-organic elements such as pearl, mineral crystals and small amounts of metals, are also frequently used.

Second, TCM is not only a medical solution to injury, infectious diseases and insanity, but also promotes life nuturing, mental health, physical strengthening and longevity. Hua Tuo, a famous doctor and surgeon in the Eastern Han Dynasty (25–220), created an effective aerobics routine to strengthen people's bones and muscles. Hua Tuo's routine (a version of Qigong), which is based on the theory of Qi, is a high-impact exercise in which the individual using it imitates the movements of the tiger, deer, ape, bear and rooster. It has been recognized by the Chinese government as a traditional exercise suitable for grass-roots promotion, and one on which fitness for all can be based.

The theory of traditional Chinese medicine is based on the well-known philosophy of the five elements — metal, wood, water, fire and earth. The five elements are

The practice of acupuncture and moxibustion therapy

Tong Ren Tang in Beijing, a Chinese pharmaceutical company founded in 1669, now the largest producer of traditional Chinese medicine

traditional Chinese philosophical terms, and in the medical field they refer to abstract concepts that represent diversifying, engendering, fluid, heat and neutralizing forces respectively. Doctors of TCM believe that the ever-lasting dynamic interactions among the five elements are reflected in the patient's physical and mental health. Hence, the best treatment of an illness is to re-establish the harmony of the five elements rather than dealing with malfunctioning of a specific organ. As a result, while treatments based on Western medical knowledge are disease-specific, the doctors of TCM adopt a patient-specific attitude and often prescribe different medicines for different patients who show the same symptoms. Hua Tuo, the doctor known for his aerobics, was also very good at treating colds. Once he received two patients who had colds. He prescribed laxatives for the first patient, who had a low fever, and a medicine to cause sweating for the other, who also had a low fever. His patients were perplexed, and he explained that his prescriptions are based on the body types rather than the disease. The laxatives could help overcome the internal deficiency in the first person's case, and the sweat-inducing prescription

could help reduce the excessive heat in the second person. The traditional diagnostic method in this medical system is fascinatingly plain, compared to modern technologies such as CT and MRI scans. A doctor studies the appearance of a patient, detects any abnormalities in his or her voice and odour, feels his or her pulse, and asks about his or her physical condition. Feeling the pulse is a common method to determine the cause of an illness, as it takes advantage of signs carried by energy meridians. It is said that signs of one's pulse are sychronized with one's physical condition. For example, a pregnant woman demonstrates a different sign in her pulse at the moment of conception.

Traditional Chinese medicine has now spread worldwide. Doctors specializing in one or more disciplines of TCM such as acupuncture, herbalism, remedy concoction and formula prescription reside in all populated continents, with a greater portion being in China, Japan, Korea and Vietnam.

牡丹 TREE PEONY

AMONG THE MANY flowers adored by the Chinese, the tree peony (*Paeonia suffruticosa*) is perhaps the most beloved. In Chinese culture, it has long been celebrated as the "Queen of Flowers", symbolizing peace and prosperity. People not only grow tree peonies in their gardens, but also express their fondness for them in various ways, such as in paintings, poems, ceramics and embroidery.

After many centuries of cultivation, the tree peony has developed into over a thousand varieties. The satiny petals can be single or double, in the shape of a water lily or chrysanthemum, and can carry golden circles or resemble joyballs. The colour also varies, and includes red, pink, white, black, blue, purple and yellow. Tree peonies can live more than a hundred years and grow slowly into shrubs that are two to seven feet (60cm–2.1m) tall. The bloom season lasts about one month, usually from mid-April to May. The tree peony looks very similar to the herbaceous peony, but unlike the latter, which dies to the ground each winter, tree peony retains its stem. By the way, in traditional Chinese medicine, the skin of its root can be used to treat many illnesses.

The tree peony is native to China and its first appearance in literature is in the *Book of Songs*, China's earliest collection of poems. Since then, it has fascinated Chinese for over 2,000 years with its voluptuous blossoms of delicate petals. Down through the centuries, poets and artists left behind a large body of splendid works about this flower, expressing their unreserved love for it. Because of its dazzling beauty, it is regarded as a symbol of femininity, luxury, lust and love. Like its Western counterpart, the rose, likenesses of the tree peony often appear on items such as clothes, hairpins, handkerchiefs, notepaper and quilts. People also associate it with national peace and prosperity as well as personal achievements in power and wealth. In this sense, the tree peony carries the wishes of the Chinese people for their country and themselves.

Today the best places to see tree peonies in China are Luoyang (in Henan Province) and Heze (in Shandong Province), which attract tourists from home and abroad during the blooming season. Tree peonies have also been introduced to many other countries and have achieved wide popularity around the world.

十二生肖 CHINESE ZODIAC

THE CHINESE ZODIAC, the "shengxiao" in Chinese, consists of twelve animals representing twelve successive years. These animals are the rat, bull, tiger, rabbit, loong, snake, horse, ram, monkey, rooster, dog and pig. The year 2009 is the Year of the Bull, which will come back again 12 years from now. The shengxiao for all babies born in 2009 is the bull.

"What animal sign were you born under?" is a way to ask about a person's age in China. In addition, as is the case with the Western zodiac, every sign represents a type of personality. For instance, people of the dog sign are generally regarded as honest, loyal, sociable and affectionate.

As a folk custom that dates back to time immemorial, the twelve animal signs leave much space for the academic world to debate their origin. There is the claim that they were passed down from the primitive ages, and a hypothesis that they were devised by the northern tribes in ancient China. And there is even the assumption that they were foreign in the first place — the signs of the zodiac may have come from ancient Babylon or another system in neighbouring India.

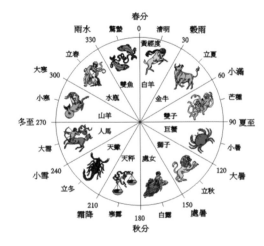

The predominant belief, however, holds that shengxiaos were as native as the Chinese ancestors who created them through the blending of totems, animal worship and astronomy.

In a country of many nationalities like China, shengxiaos are employed to record the years by various ethnic groups instead of being monopolized by Han, who, as an ethnic group, constitute about 90 percent of the Chinese population. Some even maintain that the animal signs were created by the Yi nationality in the mountains of southern China, who used a 12-animal calendar.

A belief popular among the Chinese is the concept of the Horoscope Year of one's ruling animal sign, called "ben-ming-nian" in Chinese. It is associated with the twelve animal signs and occurs every 12 years.

One's ben-ming-nian is believed to be a bad year of potential mishaps and unexpected turns. So it is advisable to ward off disasters and spin one's fortune by some means, for instance, by wearing bright red underwear or belts, a custom that is still popular today in China.

The belief that the animal signs exercise great influences on marriages was prevalent in the past and is still popular today in some parts of the country. Generally, a wedding would not take place unless an astrologist calculated the couples' shengxiaos and pronounced the marriage appropriate. The Chinese traditionally believed that only a man and a woman who had well-matched animal signs could make an ideal married couple, otherwise their marriage would not be happy.

二十四节气 24 SOLAR TERMS

THE 24 SOLAR TERMS, known in Chinese as "jieqi", mark distinct changes in the weather based on earth's position in relation to the sun. In ancient China, the solar terms played an indispensable role in agriculture, indicating the changes of the seasons and informing the cycles of planting and harvest. They reveal the ancients' sophisticated understanding of the relationships between astronomical and agricultural patterns, expressed through the simple language and vivid imagery of the twenty-four terms.

The solar terms mark 24 points each angled 15 degrees apart along the ecliptic. Two important points are the summer solstice and the winter solstice, or xiazhi and dongzhi, literally meaning "the summit of summer" and "the peak of winter". Dongzhi is also a traditional Chinese festival, held on the day of the year when the span of daylight is the shortest. It is an occasion for family reunions, where eating tangyuan (balls of glutinous rice flour) is a must, as are dumplings and chicken in some areas of the country.

The names of the solar terms vividly depict the natural phenomena associated with different times of the year. For instance, Yushui (rainwater), which starts around February 19th, suggests the appearance of rain and the coming of spring. Jingzhe, following Yushui, literally indicates the thunder awakening hibernating insects and animals. Towards the end of the year, eight solar terms successively mark the coming of cold weather — beginning with Hanlu (cold dew) and going on to Shuangjiang (the appearance of frost), Lidong (the beginning of winter), Xiaoxue (light snow), Daxue (heavy snow) and culminating with Dongzhi (the peak of winter), Xiaohan (the minor cold) and Dahan (the major cold).

This ancient drawing shows how people measured the time of each solar term with a sundial-like device.

2

NATURAL WONDERS

自然胜境

九寨沟 JIUZHAIGOU VALLEY

JIUZHAIGOU VALLEY literally means "Valley of Nine Villages," and takes its name from the nine ancient Tibetan villages that were built there. The area is a nature reserve in the north of Sichuan Province in southwestern China, and is composed of three valleys arranged in a Y shape. With majestic emerald lakes, unrivalled waterfalls, colourful forests and snow-capped peaks, all blending in great harmony, it is a jewel of nature.

Jiuzhaigou's best-known feature is its dozens of blue, green and turquoise-coloured lakes. The local Tibetan people call them "Haizi", meaning "son of the sea". Originating in glacial activity, they were dammed by rockfalls and other natural phenomena, then solidified by processes of carbonate deposition. Some lakes have a high concentration of calcium carbonate, and their water is very clear so that the bottom is often visible even at great depths. The lakes vary in colour and appearance according to their depths, mineral deposits, and surroundings. Ancient legend has it that the goddess Semo accidentally smashed her mirror, whose fragments fell down to form these beautiful lakes and streams.

Jiuzhaigou's ecosystem is classified as temperate broad-leaf forest and woodlands, much of it being virgin mixed forest. Those forests take on attractive yellow, orange, and red hues in the fall and are home to a number of interesting plant species such as varieties of rhododendron and bamboo. The local fauna includes the endangered giant panda and golden snub-nosed monkey. Both populations are very small and isolated.

Jiuzhaigou's landscape is made up of high-altitude karsts shaped by glacial, hydrological and tectonic activity. This remote region was inhabited by various Tibetan and Qiang peoples for centuries, but was not officially discovered by the government until 1972. Its highest point, located at the end of the valley, is 15,420ft (4,700m) above sea level.

青海湖 LAKE QINGHAI

THE NAME QINGHAI literally means "Blue Sea". At a height of 10,500ft (3,200m) above sea level, Qinghai Lake is not only the largest inland saltwater lake in China, but also the largest mountain lake of Central Asia. Its remote peacefulness and association with Tibetan Buddhism make it one of the sacred destinations for pilgrims.

Qinghai Lake is located on the Tibetan plateau in northwestern China. It is 65 miles (105km) long and 40 miles (64km) wide. According to geologists, the lake was formed during the Late Pleistocene Epoch by water from melting glaciers.

The surrounding grassland and green mountains add to the purity of water an idyllic and peaceful flavour, which is believed to be helpful for meditation. Against the blue sky and white clouds, the lake looks especially charming and amazing. Migratory birds usually choose this place as an intermediate stop on their migration routes, and so in spring and summer many rare species can be seen there. On the western side of the lake there is a peninsula, called Bird Island. It is now a wildlife reserve inhabited by more than 100,000 birds, hence the name. Campers, tourists, bird watchers, poets and nomads are all attracted to Qinghai Lake by its biodiversity and calm.

At the centre of the lake, there is a small island which used to be a holy place. According to legend, a Buddhist temple there was visited by a large number of worshippers every winter when the lake was frozen. They were prohibited from entering the island and monsters in the temple were prohibited from going out to the mainland during summer because no boat was used at that time. Today, many religious people still regard this lake as a holy place for spiritual transcendence. They would like to complete the circuit around the lake by horse or on foot, which takes almost one month to finish.

日月潭 LAKE SUN MOON

SUN MOON LAKE is the largest natural lake in China's Taiwan Province and one of the few mountain lakes in China. Around the lake lives an aboriginal tribe.

More than 2,300ft (700m) above sea level, Sun Moon Lake is surrounded by green mountains and scenic countryside. It is said that the lake was hidden from the outside world until it was found by a group of hunters tracking a deer, who were astonished by its beauty. The lake is a tourist attraction and a favourite wedding place, and its crystal-clear waters are filled with a romantic atmosphere.

In the middle of the lake is a small island called Lalu, an original habitation for the Cao people, a branch of the local aborigines. During the Japanese occupation, a hydroelectric station was built on the island and the Cao were forced out, but they still live around the lake.

Lalu Island cut the lake into two parts. The northern part is named Sun Lake and the southern part Moon Lake, because one is shaped like the sun and the other like a new moon. There is also a folk story about how the lake got its name. Once upon a time, Sun Moon Lake was a big pond inhabited by two evil dragons. One day the male dragon jumped up and swallowed the sun and that night the female dragon swallowed the moon. When darkness fell, a couple of hunters found the dragons, hitting their heads and cutting their stomachs with scissors to let the sun and the moon out to rise to the sky. While people on earth were welcoming the regained brightness, the two dragons turned into a lake round like a sun and a lake shaped like a crescent respectively.

Every year, aboriginal clans in the Sun Moon Lake region hold a harvest festival, a sowing festival, and special handicraft fairs at which cultural articles can be found.

峨眉山 MOUNT EMEI

LOCATED IN SICHUAN Province in western China, Emei Mountain occupies an exalted place in Chinese Buddhist culture. Famed for its spectacular natural beauty, the mountain range boasts misty green forests, sparkling waterfalls, and winding ridges and peaks whose shape and beauty resemble "fair eyebrows" (after which the mountain is named).

Mount Emei is one of the Four Sacred Buddhist Mountains in China. It is said that Buddhism was first established here and then spread east. The patron bodhisattva of the mountain is Samantabhadra, known in Chinese Buddhism as Puxian, who embodies virtue and asceticism. Today, the mountain remains a major pilgrimage destination.

Purportedly, the first Buddhist temple in China was built on Mount Emei during the 1st century AD. Some two hundred temples and monasteries have been erected since, and over the centuries, Mount Emei has become a cherished repository of Buddhist architecture. The seventy or so existing temples, most of which were built during the Ming (1368–1644) and Qing (1616–1911) dynasties, display highly versatile architectural styles adapting to the terrain, differing from traditional Buddhist monastic structures. Interestingly, structures such as the Fuhu ("vanquish the tigers") Temple reveal Taoist influences, and it is believed that martial arts were practiced on the mountain during the 16th and 17th centuries.

Mount Emei is rich and diverse in vegetation and wildlife, with millennium-old trees and many endangered animals, including pandas. Subtropical and subalpine forests are both found here, and among the rare plant species, the dove tree (*Davidia involucrata*) and the spinulose tree fern (*Cyathea spinulosa*) are known as living fossils for their ancient provenance. Because of its ecological diversity, Mount Emei is also known as the "Kingdom of Plants and Paradise for Animals". During the Permian period it was a volcanic area, and today the region is geologically known as the Mount Emei Igneous Province.

At the summit, which is 10,167ft (3,099m) above sea level, lucky visitors will observe several natural phenomena known as Mount Emei's four great wonders: the sea of clouds; the sunrise; the so-called "Buddhist halo", an iridescent ring that appears around the shadow of the observer in the clouds; and the "holy lamps", flickering lights that are said to hover amidst the ravines on moonless nights. Mount Emei was named a UNESCO World Heritage Site in 1996 for its "exceptional cultural significance" and "natural beauty into which the human element has been integrated" (UNESCO).

黄山 MOUNT HUANG (YELLOW MOUNTAIN)

LOCATED IN ANHUI Province in eastern China, Mount Huang, or the Yellow Mountain, has been renowned throughout the centuries for its beautiful scenery. It is named after the Yellow Emperor, the mythical ancestor of Chinese civilization, who is said to have once lived and gathered herbal medicine here. The earliest known reference to the connection between the mountain and the Emperor was made by the great poet Li Bai (701–762).

The Yellow Mountain was formed approximately 100 million years ago, shaped by stratum uplift and glacial movement. Today, Lotus Peak, Bright Summit Peak and Celestial Peak are its three tallest peaks. Among the mountain's distinct features are stone pillar forests and peculiarly shaped granite peaks, and the elusive mist after the rain, which has enchanted painters and calligraphers since times of old. Indeed, with its precarious drops and dramatic rises, dotted by gnarled, ancient pine trees and strewn with spectacular pools and waterfalls, the Yellow Mountain appears straight out of a painting.

Among the Yellow Mountain's many ancient trees, the loong-shaped "Welcome Pine" has become symbolic of it, greeting visitors today as it did thirteen centuries ago. And visitors continue to ascend the 60,000-odd stone steps up the lengths of the peaks, parts of which are said to be over 1,500 years old.

Throughout history, the Yellow Mountain has inspired countless writers, calligraphers and painters, including masters of the landscape schools of traditional Chinese waterpainting. The modern Chinese painter Liu Haisu once compared the mountain to "the most natural and most beautiful traditional ink painting".

The Yellow Mountain was declared a UNESCO World Heritage site in 1990, and a site of Scenic Beauty and Historic Interest by the Chinese government. In 2006, then-UN Secretary-General Kofi Annan named a pine tree on the Yellow Mountain "Umbrella Pine".

庐山 MOUNT LU

MOUNT LU, with its rich cultural heritage and beautiful natural landscape, is a UNESCO World Heritage site in southeast China. It was formerly and still is a summer resort, an education centre and a religious place for its outstanding aesthetic value and status as one of the spiritual origins of Chinese civilization.

Situated on the south bank of the Yangtze River and facing Poyang Lake, Mount Lu is enshrouded in mist all year round, and is much cooler than the surrounding region. In the summer, people love retreating to the mountain to escape the heat. In addition, the grand and steep peaks (their highest point is almost a mile above sea level) and the majestic waterfalls, together with the impressive views along the valleys, encourage people to discover their unmatched beauty.

In the Tang Dynasty (618–907), the poet Li Bo retired to Mount Lu and raised white deer there. Later, his place of seclusion was turned into an academy, known as White Deer Cavern Academy, which gradually became one of the four higher learning institutes in ancient China. In the Song Dynasty (960–1279), Zhu Xi, one of the most eminent Confucian scholars and influential philosophers in China, meditated for years and developed the *School of Principle* there.

Mount Lu is also a religious marvel. It is the birthplace of the Pure Land Sect of Buddhism, one of the most popular Buddhist sects in China. In the 4th century, Huiyuan, founder of the sect, set up a monastery on Mount Lu to preach his doctrines. It is said that he never left Mount Lu all his life. Besides its strong relationship with the development of Buddhism in China, Mount Lu is also a centre of other religions. It is amazing that Buddhist and Taoist temples, Islamic mosques and Christian churches can all be found there.

珠穆朗玛峰 MOUNT QOMOLANGMA (MOUNT EVEREST)

MOUNT QOMOLANGMA, also known as Mount Everest, is the highest mountain on earth, its summit being 29,017ft (8,844m) above sea level. The highest peak in the Himalayan Ranges, it is located on the border between Nepal and China. Qomolangma literally means Mother Goddess of the World. It is regarded as Saint Mother in China. The Chinese name Qomolangma was marked on a Chinese map more than 280 years ago.

Streaming flag clouds are the symbolic sight of Mount Qomolangma. The ivory clouds float like flying flags over the summit. Local people call the flag clouds the world's highest weather vane, because they can judge whether the wind is strong or not by the cloud shapes.

The rocks on Mount Qomolangma have been subdivided into three formations by geologists. From the summit to the base are the Qomolangma Formation, the North Col Formation and the Rongbuk Formation. Glaciers are another feature of Mount Qomolangma, with Rongbuk Glacier being the most famous. However, due to the process of global warming, glaciers on the mountain are shrinking fast and are in danger of extinction.

The Qomolangma National Nature Reserve was established in 1989. It covers an area of 13,127 square miles (34,000sq.km) centred on Mount Qomolangma. It is renowned for its high biological diversity and natural beauty. The Chinese government has banned hunting and the trafficking of wild animals there since 1989. Some endangered animal species such as snow leopard, lynx and wolf live in this preserved area. In 1999, the Qomolangma Nature Reserve was recognized by the United Nations as one of the world's most successful examples of sustainable development.

For several centuries, the Himalayas and Mount Qomolangma have been regarded as a sacred place. Local residents believe that the Goddess of the Earth lives in Mount Qomolangma. Her steed is an ox and sometimes is seen to be a tiger. According to Buddhists, they may gain an understanding of the world and journey toward

enlightenment on Mount Qomolangma. Rongbuk Monastery is located on the northern slope of the mountain. At 16,909ft (5,154m) above sea level, it is the highest monastery in the world. Built in 1899, the monastery has always been a place for local people to pray and seek blessings. Now it serves as a base camp for climbing the summit.

Climbers from all over the world cannot resist the temptation of conquering the summit of Mount Qomolangma. However, altitude sickness, weather and wind present threatening challenges for climbers. The first human ascent of the summit was accomplished in 1953. Seven years later, the first Chinese climbing team succeeded in reaching the summit.

On May 8, 2008, the Olympic flame and the Olympic flag made their trip to the summit of Mount Qomolangma. This unprecedented Olympic torch relay on the highest site on earth lasted about six minutes and was recorded forever in the history of the Olympic Games.

泰山 MOUNT TAI

MOUNT TAI IS THE FOREMOST of China's Five Sacred Mountains, and was included on the UNESCO's World Heritage List as early as in 1987. Located in central Shandong Province, it rises abruptly from the vast plain of northern China, attracting tourists with its natural beauty and cultural richness.

Mount Tai presents tourists with a picturesque landscape of cliffs, forests, springs, and waterfalls as it pierces upward into the sky in a towering and majestic manner. Jade Emperor Peak, the main peak, reaches an altitude of 5,069ft (1,545m) with fascinating rocks and cliffs alive with chattering springs and roaring waterfalls. The water was known as "Divine Water" in the old days — modern scientific analysis shows it is rich in many trace elements that are essential for human health.

Mount Tai is very famous for its trees — in fact, vegetation covers 80 percent of the mountain. The oldest and most notable trees include the Han Dynasty Cypresses planted by Emperor Wu 2,100 years ago.

The mountain itself is integral to Chinese civilization — religion, arts and letters in particular. It is a holy place for Taoism, Buddhism and Confucianism, the three major philosophies of Chinese thinking. Many accomplished Buddhists and Taoists considered Mount Tai as the ideal place for religious cultivation. Confucius, the founder of Confucianism, gave many lectures on Mount Tai.

The charm of Mount Tai also lies in its links with imperial power; despite the rise and fall of dynasties, this mountain remained as a symbol of the empire. So much so that emperors came and held elaborate ceremonies to pay homage to Heaven and Earth here.

The beauty of Mount Tai has appealed to generations of top artists and scholars, who left behind them a considerable legacy of masterpieces celebrating the mountain, including more than 819 stone tablets and 1,018 cliff-side and stone inscriptions. Among them is the huge inscription of *Diamond Sutra*, a Buddhist classic, in the Sutra Rock Valley.

武当山 MOUNT WUDANG

MOUNT WUDANG, situated in Hubei Province, is known for its spectacular natural scenery and legendary associations with Chinese Taoist culture. According to myth, Wudang martial arts originated from the Taoist master Zhang Sanfeng, who became inspired by the battle between a cobra and a white crane. Today, Taoist monks continue to inhabit the temple complexes scattered on the steep inclines of the mountain, while the floating mist, deep ravines and dense forests give the place a mystical aura.

Mount Wudang attracted Taoist visitors as early as the Eastern Han Dynasty (25–220), and the first site of worship was built several centuries later, during the Tang Dynasty (618–907). In the Ming Dynasty elaborate monastery complexes were built, beginning in 1412 with construction completed twelve years later. The existing monasteries, outstanding examples the architectural styles of the Yuan, Ming and Qing dyansties, served as centres for religious study, meditative practice and the practice of Taoist martial arts. In the Wudang tradition, the cultivation of morality served as the basis of physical practice, whether it was sword-fighting or taiji. Agility in movement and making use of the opponent's strength were core components of the sword-fighting practice.

Mount Wudang boasts extraordinary ecological diversity within its area of 154 square miles (400sq.km). According to one of the most renowned botanists and pharmacists, Li Shizhen, one third of all the medicinal herbs which he recorded in his vast compendium were collected on the mountain, which has since acquired its reputation as a natural herbary. The highest peak, Heavenly Pillar Peak, rises 5,289ft (1,612m) above sea level; its name means "column supporting the sky".

In 1994, the ancient building complexes on the mountain became listed as a UNESCO World Heritage site. The film *Crouching Tiger, Hidden Dragon*, partly shot on the mountain, helped to popularize Wudang martial arts. Today, biannual traditional martial arts festivals are held here, and visitors ascend the stone steps in wonder.

武夷山 MOUNT WUYI

MOUNT WUYI is a mountain range located along the border of Fujian Province with Jiangxi Province in China. The mountain range covers an area of 23 square miles (60sq.km).

Mount Wuyi was listed as a UNESCO World Heritage site in 1999, both natural and cultural. It is known for its natural beauty and ancient Chinese cultural tradition.

As one of the most distinguished subtropical forests in the world and the refuge for ancient, relict plant species and large numbers of reptile, amphibian and insect species, Mount Wuyi is the most outstanding biodiversity conservation zone in southeastern China. The landscape is characterized by winding river valleys, dome-shaped cliffs and mysterious caves. Peaks generally consist of volcanic or plutonic rocks. With its exceptional scenic beauty, the Nine-Bend River is a typical attraction for tourists. The most popular activity for tourists is a raft trip down the river. The mountain area is free from industrial pollution, so the Chinese government set up its first air quality monitoring station here in 2005.

Human traces here date back 4,000 years, judging from archaeological remains. The earliest cotton fabrics in China were found in the boat coffins there. The Hongqiao boards and the ancient capital city of the Minyue kingdom — established in the 1st century BC – are both evidence of ancient civilization and traditional customs. These early settlements gradually developed the Gumin and the Minyue cultures. However both of them have vanished in the long expanse of history.

Mount Wuyi was first a centre of Taoism, and later Buddhism also took root here. Taoist temples and Buddhist monasteries have been built from the Northern Song (960–1127) to the Qing Dynasty (1616–1911). However, most of these buildings are very incomplete today. The mountain was also the cradle of Neo-Confucianism. The most important representatives of this trend are Chen Yi (1033–1107), Chen Hao (1033–1085) and Zhu Xi (1130–1200).

Neo-Confucianism was the dominant intellectual theory from the Song to the Qing dynasties. It represented the traditional national ideology of China, and has been influential in eastern and southeastern Asian countries since the 11th century. The influence of Neo-Confucianism has also spread to the philosophy and government of much of the world. Zhu Xi, the greatest representative of Neo-Confucianism and one of the most influential figures in Chinese traditional culture, further developed traditional Confucian theories.

Mount Wuyi is the origin of the world famous Da Hong Pao tea. Many different types of tea are produced in the area of Mount Wuyi.

A tourist raft negotiates one of the bends on the Nine-Bend River

漓江 RIVER LI

THE LI RIVER is a tributary of the Pearl River system in southern China's Guangxi Province. It is 272 miles (437km) long and famous for its beautiful scenery, its unusual topography and its influence on early Chinese history.

Its course from Guilin City to Yangshuo City is one of China's most beautiful scenic areas. The river winds like a green silk belt among mountain chains, with peaks on both sides rising high into the sky. For thousands of years, the breathtaking scenery has been admired as a 62 mile (100km) long Chinese ink painting scroll. It is one of China's top tourist destinations, and the beautiful scenery is printed on the 20 RMB banknote.

Elephant Trunk Hill is the symbol of the Li River scenery and there is a beautiful legend about the pagoda on the hill. An elephant worked so hard for the Emperor of Heaven that he fell ill, so the local farmers took care of him until he recovered. Being grateful, he stayed and helped them. The Emperor was annoyed and thrust his sword into the elephant's back and turned the elephant into the rocky hill. The sword later became the famous pagoda.

The Li River basin is famous for its green mountains, transparent river flow, wonderful caves and unique stones. The peaks along the river are extraordinarily beautiful. On February 11, 2008, UNESCO and the Chinese government signed an agreement on establishing the International Research Centre on Karst in Guilin, the famous tourist city along the river.

The Li River also had profound cultural and military influence in Chinese history. It is recorded that Lingqu (literally "Spiritual Ditch") Canal, dug in 214 BC, was the earliest canal in both China and the world. It was constructed to connect the Li River and the Xiang River, by order of the Emperor Qin Shi Huang, to unite the southern part of China politically and economically.

The Li River on a 20-RMB banknote

长江 RIVER YANGTZE

THE THIRD-LONGEST RIVER in the world, after the Nile and the Amazon, the Yangtze is the longest river in China, with a length of over 3,700 miles (6,000km). The name Yangtze actually refers only to the lower part of this long river, whose real name in Chinese is "Chang Jiang", which means "Long River". Since "Yangtze" was the first name for it to be heard by the Western missionaries and traders in China, they mistook it for the name of the whole river.

From its source in Qinghai Province, in the Tanggula Mountains of the Tibetan plateau, the Yangtze flows eastward to the East China Sea (part of the Pacific Ocean).

Like the Yellow River, the Yangtze is also a cradle of ancient Chinese civilization, with human activities tracing back as far as 27,000 years ago. The representative cultures along the river are the Bashu near the upper Yangtze, the Jingchu in the middle reach, and the Wuyue in the lower Yangtze. Today, the Yangtze remains among the busiest waterways in China and in the world, nourishing a number of China's largest and most important cities including Chongqing, Wuhan, Nanjing, and Shanghai at its mouth. The Sichuan Basin and the Yangtze Basin are among the most fertile regions in the country, while the Yangtze River Delta is now China's most important industrial area.

The river looms large in the Chinese cultural landscape. Historically, many battles took place along the Yangtze, which served as the dividing line between northern and southern China, both strategically and culturally. The marvellous and varied landscape along the river appears in many poems and paintings, and indeed, many rock inscriptions still lie scattered along its shores.

The Three Gorges, perhaps the best-known scenic site along the Yangtze, marks a spectacular 125 mile (200km) stretch along the middle course of the river. With the river roaring through steep valleys, narrowly flanked on both sides by near-vertical peaks, the Three Gorges has enchanted visitors since times of old. The Three Gorges Dam, among the world's largest hydroelectric power complexes, lies near the Xilingxia Gorge.

The Yangtze's most dramatic site in southern China is Tiger Leaping Gorge, one of the world's deepest and narrowest river canyons. According to folklore, a tiger being chased by hunters leapt across the canyon at the river's narrowest crossing point. Near this stretch, the Yangtze flows parallel to the Mekong and Salween rivers, surrounded by snowy peaks, in an area known as the Three Parallel Rivers of Yunnan Protected Areas, designated a UNESCO World Heritage site in 2003.

The Yangtze boasts rich ecological diversity. It is home to the finless porpoise, the world's only freshwater porpoise, and the baiji, the Yangtze River dolphin. These intelligent, rare creatures are both on the brink of extinction, and conservationists are taking active steps to help preserve their vanishing natural habitats.

Sunset along the Three Gorges on the Yangtze River

香格里拉 SHANGRI-LA

THE LEGEND of Shangri-la tells of a mystical kingdom hidden among snowy peaks, an earthly paradise unknown to the outside world. Drawing on the legend, the British writer James Hilton popularized the mystical town of Shangri-la in his 1933 novel *Lost Horizon*, which described its location as somewhere in the western end of the Kunlun Mountains in southwest China.

Today, Shangri-La appears as a place on a map, a popular tourist destination in northwestern Yunnan Province — a town formerly named Zhongdian, officially renamed in 2001 after the town in the novel. Situated at 10,760ft (3,280m) above sea level, Shangri-La lies amid spectacular natural scenery. The glaciated peaks of Meili, Baima and Haba mountains form a dramatic skyline in the distance, with the highest peak, Kawagebo, rising 22,113ft (6,740m) above sea level. Near the Meili mountains, the Mingyong Glacier, at 8,858ft (2,700m) above sea level, is one of the lowest-lying glaciers in the northern hemisphere.

Against the backdrop of the snowy peaks, three of the great rivers of Asia — the Yangtze, Mekong and Salween — run parallel for some 106 miles (170km) in this part of Yunnan through a protected area of 4.2 million acres (1.7 million hectares). The area has been listed as a UNESCO World Heritage site for its biodiversity and geological significance, with landscapes that range from Himalayan to tropical along its 19,685ft (6,000m) gradient.

Shangri-La lies in an area of extraordinary cultural diversity, populated by more than ten ethnic groups such as the Han, Tibetan, Naxi, Bai, Yi and Lisu, who have imbued the natural surroundings with vivid stories and myths. In the vicinity of the town, the wetland preserve of Napahai is the winter home to rare black-necked cranes, regarded by the Tibetans as spirits symbolizing joy and good fortune. Also near the town, the Gedansongzanlin Lamasery is a Tibetan lamasery decorated with golden statues and beautiful frescoes.

About 60 miles (100km) south of the town, the White Water Terrace is a sacred Naxi site, featuring limestone hills and cascades of calcium carbonate deposits, where spirits are said to dwell. Local Naxi residents come here for worship and prayer, throwing rice grains in veneration. Dongba, the language of the Naxi, is the world's only living pictorial language.

Sangri-la evokes the image of a serene utopia, which attracts millions of tourists every year.

石林 STONE FOREST

STONE FOREST is a large group of karst limestone formations in southwest China. With a history of 200 to 300 million years, it covers an area of 154 square miles (400sq.km) featuring peaks, pillars, stalagmites, underground rivers and caves. From a distance, the whole landscape looks like a huge forest.

Walking through the Stone Forest, one would be thrilled by the magical power of nature and the magnificent stone formations. Stones arise abruptly from the ground, looking like animals, plants or even humans. Geologists say that nearly 270 million years ago, during the Carboniferous period of the Paleozoic era, this region was an expanse of ocean. Later, due to constant geographical movements, the waters dried up and a wonderful limestone landscape emerged. Exposed to the corrosive power of nature, rough stones of various sizes became what they appear today.

Behind every stone pinnacle there is a beautiful story, usually associated with the Sani people living around this region generation after generation. One pinnacle, resembling a slim and pretty girl, is called Ashma, the heroine of an epic poem told for thousands of years among the Sani people. Ashma was a Sani girl who refused to be married to a local landlord. She ran away from the wedding and fought against the landlord with her lover, Ahei. When they came to the Stone Forest they were finally discovered by the landlord, who summoned up a flood and drowned Ashma. The poor girl turned into a stone and evaded the fate of being captured.

Each year on the 24th of the sixth lunar month, the Sani people celebrate the Torch Festival, which attracts visitors from home and abroad. The Sani youngsters take part in folk dances, wrestling, bullfighting, pole-climbing and loong-playing around the Stone Forest. Visitors are welcome to attend these traditional celebrations and share the happiness.

西湖 WEST LAKE IN HANGZHOU

WHEN THE ITALIAN EXPLORER Marco Polo first arrived in Hangzhou seven centuries ago, he was charmed by the beautiful West Lake, and described this Chinese city as the greatest in the world. With its willow-lined banks and shores dotted with engravings, tea houses and historical sites, the lake continues to play an important role in the city's cultural and recreational life.

The West Lake has occupied an important place in Chinese literary culture, particularly during the Southern Song Dynasty (1127–1279), when the dynastic capital was shifted from Kaifeng to Hangzhou. The great poet Su Dongpo (1037–1101) once compared the West Lake to Xi Zi, the most beautiful woman in ancient China; indeed, the lake also became known as the Xizi Lake.

Perhaps the best-known legend associated with the West Lake is that of the White Snake. As the story goes, the White Snake was a serpentine spirit who longed for the mortal world, and transformed herself into a beautiful maiden on her way to the West Lake. At the Broken Bridge by the lake, she met and fell in love with the handsome yet faint-hearted Xu Xian. Their love was eventually undermined by the monk Fahai, who revealed to Xu the snake's true identity, leading him to betray her, and imprisoned her under the Thunder Peak Pagoda.

Today, the Thunder Peak Pagoda and the Broken Bridge are two of the lake's ten famed sites. Each site is designated by a four-character epithet, and when combined these reveal the charms of the lake through the seasons, at different times of day:

The vernal dawn at the Su causeway
The wind-rippled lotus pond by the winery
The autumnal moon over the still lake
The remnant snow on the Broken Bridge
The Thunder Peak Pagoda at sunset
The Twin Peaks, piercing the clouds
In the wind-swept willows, the warbling orioles
At the Flower Pond, the koi to be admired
The moon, mirrored in the three lakes
The evening bell, resounding on Nanping Hill

Divided by three causeways and surrounded by hills on three sides, the West Lake is today a freshwater lake covering an area of approximately 2.5 square miles (6.5sq.km). Among its wonders is the famous Longjing Tea, nourished by the water from a nearby spring.

West of the lake, the National Tea Museum hosts exhibits on the cultural history of Chinese tea. Near the southern bank of the lake, the National Silk Museum is the largest of its kind and hosts comprehensive exhibits on Chinese silk culture.

黄河 YELLOW RIVER

THE YELLOW RIVER is China's mother river. The Yellow Emperor, the mythical founder of Chinese civilization, is said to have ruled in the Yellow River Basin. It is also here, once the most prosperous agricultural region in the Middle Kingdom, that northern Chinese civilization is believed to have been born. Along the river, Xi'an and Luoyang are two major cities which had each been dynastic capitals for more than a thousand years.

With a total length of 3,395 miles (5,464km), the Yellow River is the second longest in China after the Yangtze. Originating in the Bayan Har Mountains in western China, it descends the Qinghai-Tibet Plateau and loops north, then dramatically bends south before flowing east to its mouth at the Bohai Sea. In early records, the Yellow River is simply referred to as "the River". It is called the "Yellow River" because sections of it are laden with loess deposits, which give it a yellow tint.

Along the middle course of the Yellow River, the Hukou Waterfall is the second largest in China and the only yellow waterfall in the world. Excessive erosion along this part of the river has led to the accumulation of sediment downstream, and the elevated river bed has caused a number of devastating floods. Throughout history, the river has changed its main course eighteen times, often with drastic implications for the inhabitants along its shores. Today, several hydroelectric dams have been constructed along the river, while efforts continue to battle erosion and control flooding.

The rich and varied cultural traditions that developed along different sections of the Yellow River include the waist drum dance, the Nadam fair, the silhouette puppet theatre and the river lantern festival. Cave dwellings and water cellars are also found along the river. In the modern era, the river has been memorialized by two large-scale musical compositions, the *Yellow River Cantata* and the *Yellow River Piano Concerto*.

3

ARCHITECTURAL HERITAGE

人文景观

苏州园林 CLASSICAL GARDENS OF SUZHOU

WHILE THE IMPERIAL GARDENS of the Forbidden City in Beijing embody the palace garden tradition, the classical gardens of Suzhou, a major historic city of eastern China, represent the private garden tradition of China, which has also exerted great influence in some other Asian countries. The Suzhou tradition also served as a model for the Astor Court in the New York Metropolitan Museum of Art.

Suzhou has been blessed with prosperity for over a thousand years. During the Ming and Qing dynasties (14th to 20th centuries), Suzhou was the home of intellectuals and wealthy merchants who strongly influenced Chinese culture. They built gardens to express their attitude toward life and to compete with each other for prestige.

Suzhou boasts a history of gardens dating back more than 2,600 years. Only about 200 remain, of which the four most renowned are Zhuozheng Garden (the Humble Administrator's Garden), Canglang Pavilion (the Blue Waves Pavilion), Liu Garden (Lingering Garden), and Shizi Grove (Lions Grove).

The beauty of the classical Chinese garden is different from that of Western gardens. While Chinese gardens evoke the essence of nature, the classical Western gardens reproduce nature based on principles of order and rationality. This contrast encourages us to reflect on the infinite possibility of beauty and to create beauty reflecting images of paradise.

Although most of private gardens of Suzhou are small, with an average area of 12,000 square yards (10,000sq.m), their delicate design reflects the metaphysical importance of natural beauty. Whether on a bright spring day or a cool autumn night, people would gather to share their affections with family and friends, to compose poetry, and to admire paintings. They would enjoy music, play chess, and meet lovers under the moon. Imagining these scenes, we can better appreciate the poetic sensibilities of the gardeners who created these urban mountains and forests.

To build a garden is to build a paradise. Gardens are intended to be peaceful retreats and resting places for the weary. Standing there now, we not only see pavilions, pagodas, terraces, mountains, waters, flowers and grass, but also sense what Chinese of centuries past appreciated and believed. From Taoism the gardens incorporated the concept of letting things take their own course, imitating the natural flow of mountains and forests. From Confucianism they took a sense of idealism reflected in the mountains and waters. From Buddhism they borrowed the practice of meditation, filling gardens with linden trees to provide places for quiet contemplation. Incorporating Chinese cultural traditions, they embedded carved stone inscriptions in corridor walls, keeping the wisdom of their ancestors alive.

When the classical gardens of Suzhou were added to the World Heritage list in 1997, the organizing committee remarked, "The four classical gardens of Suzhou are masterpieces of Chinese landscape garden design in which art, nature, and ideas are integrated perfectly to create ensembles of great beauty and peaceful harmony, and the four gardens are integral to the entire historic urban plan."

故宫 FORBIDDEN CITY

THE FORBIDDEN CITY, also named the Palace Museum, is the most magnificent and splendid palace complex in China. The construction took 14 years and was finished in 1420, 14 years before Shakespeare was born. In the Ming Dynasty and the Qing Dynasty (1616–1911), it was the imperial palace where 24 emperors ascended the throne and exercised their strong power over the nation.

The huge palace occupies an area of 861,100 square yards (720,000sq.m) and has approximately 8,700 rooms. A high red wall with a total length of 11,155ft (3,400m) encases the rectangular palace. There is a gate in each side, with Meridian Gate (Wu Men) as the main entrance, and four exquisite watchtowers sit at the corners of the wall. With roofs covered with golden glazed tiles, red-painted walls and grey-white bases, the palace appears extremely luxurious and grand. Spectacular halls in it are neatly arranged in symmetry along a central axis that conforms to the axis of Beijing City.

The palace has two primary parts: the Outer Court and the Inner Court. The former consists of the first three main halls, where the emperor received his courtiers and conducted grand ceremonies, while the latter was the living quarters for the empror. Some halls are now converted into art galleries to exhibit paintings, clocks, bronze wares, pottery and other invaluable treasures. It is said that there are over one million articles in the palace.

The main entrance to the palace is the Meridian Gate, which was so named because the emperor considered himself the "Son of Heaven" and the palace the centre of the universe, and so the north-south axis going right through the palace was thought of as the Meridian Line.

Beyond the Meridian Gate unfolds a vast courtyard across which the Inner Golden Water River runs from east to west. The river is spanned by five bridges, which were the symbols of the five virtues preached by Confucius — benevolence, righteousness, rites, intelligence and fidelity.

At the north end of the courtyard is a three-tiered white marble terrace, 23ft (7m) above the ground, on which, one after another, stand three majestic halls: the Hall of Supreme Harmony, the Hall of Complete Harmony and the Hall of Preserving Harmony.

The rectangular Hall of Supreme Harmony is 89ft

(27m) in height, and 2,751 square yards (2,300sq.m) in area, and is the grandest and most important hall in the palace complex. It is also China's largest existing wooden palace and an outstanding example of brilliant colour combinations. This hall used to be the throne hall for ceremonies that marked great occasions: the Winter Solstice, the Spring Festival, the emperor's birthday and the dispatch of generals to battles, etc. On such occasions there would be an imperial guard of honour standing in front of the Hall that extended all the way to the Meridian Gate.

At the rear of the Inner Court is the Imperial Garden where the emperor and his family could relax. The Imperial Garden was laid out during the early Ming Dynasty. Hundreds of pines and cypresses offer shade while various flowers give colours to the garden all year round and fill the air with their fragrance.

The Hall of Complete Harmony (Zhong He Dian), the smallest of the three main halls in the Outer Court in the Forbidden City

The Hall of Supreme Harmony (Tai He Dian), the largest hall within the Forbidden City

京杭大运河 GRAND CANAL

THE GRAND CANAL OF CHINA is the longest artificial river of the ancient world. Stretching for 1,115 miles (1,794km), it is located in eastern China, running from Beijing to Hangzhou while passing through Tianjin and the provinces of Hebei, Shandong, Jiangsu and Zhejiang. While most natural rivers, including the Yangtze and Yellow rivers, flow from west to east, the Grand Canal runs north to south, connecting urban centres in China throughout the ages.

Construction of the Grand Canal dates back to the Spring and Autumn Period (770–476 BC). Fuchai, king of the Wu Kingdom (in present-day Suzhou), had conquered the neighbouring kingdom of Qi. He ordered the construction of a canal to transport his armies and supplies to the north, lest he should engage the northern states. Work began in 486 BC in the city of Han (in present-day Yangzhou in Jiangsu Province), and this section of the canal was named Han Gou. It was about 93 miles (150km) long, connecting the Yangtze River and the Huai River.

The main section of the Grand Canal was built during the Sui Dynasty (581–618), when the agricultural centre of China had moved from the Yellow River valley to present-day Jiangsu and Zhejiang Provinces. Emperor Wen launched the massive project, which was carried forward by his successor Emperor Yang from 604 to 609, mobilizing a labour force of 5 million. The completed canal, stretching more than 1,240 miles (2,000km), had a Y shape that connected present-day Hangzhou, Luoyang and Beijing. The main function of the canal during the Tang Dynasty (618–907) — and throughout the following dynasties — was to reduce the cost of transporting taxed grain from the Yangtze River Delta to northern China.

Among the cities that prospered from the construction of the Grand Canal was Yangzhou, which witnessed the economic boom of the Tang Dynasty. Situated close to the canal, it was the centre of the government's salt monopoly and lay on the geographical midpoint of the south-north trade axis.

During the Yuan Dynasty (1206–1368), the capital city was moved to Dadu (present-day Beijing). In order to avoid a detour, a summit section was dug across the foothills of Shandong Province during the 1280s, linking Hangzhou and Beijing by a direct north-south waterway for the first time. Thus the overall length of the canal was reduced by as much as 435 miles (700km).

Historically, the function of the Grand Canal was frequently disrupted by periodic flooding of the Yellow River. During wartime, the dikes of the Yellow River were sometimes deliberately broken to inundate advancing enemy troops, causing disasters and prolonged economic difficulties in the flooded regions. Ruined and dilapidated from time to time, the Grand Canal was reconstructed and repaired a number of times.

长城 GREAT WALL

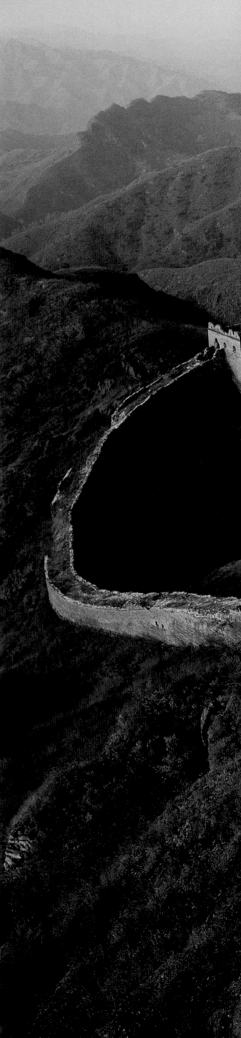

THE FOUNDER OF THE Qin Dynasty, Emperor Qin Shi Huang, ended the period of the Warring States (475–221 BC) by uniting his fractured nation. After that, he began to piece together the independent defensive walls of the different states in an effort to build the longest wall in the world, which would protect China's northern border. The 4,000 mile (6,400km) long Great Wall was a colossal defence engineering project, and at the time it was also regarded as strategically invincible with its huge numbers of impressive fortifications. Even if one of the fortifications was seized by the enemy, the bright fire and dense smoke on the beacon tower on top of the fortification would relay the message of emergency so quickly that the main army would hurry to the spot and quickly subdue the invasion.

Starting out in the east on the banks of the Yalu River in Liaoning Province, the Great Wall stretches westwards to Jiayuguan Pass in the desert. It is known as the Ten Thousand Li Wall in China. The Wall climbs up and down, and twists and turns along the ridges of the Yinshan Mountain, like a giant necklace on a background of green velvet. However, during its construction tens of thousands of labourers lost their lives and were buried beneath the wall.

There is no shortage of legends about the wall, and one of the favourite stories concerns the bitter experience of a woman named Meng Jiangnü. It tells of her husband, Fan Xiliang, who was arrested by federal officials and sent to build the wall. When Meng Jiangnü had heard nothing from him for years, she set out to look for him. Unfortunately, by the time she reached the wall, her husband had already died of toil and hunger. Hearing the bad news, she cried her heart out and her wailing was so loud and heartbreaking that a section of the Great Wall collapsed.

Much of the ancient wall is badly damaged and even missing, owing to weathering and disintegration — after all, the Great Wall has witnessed the rise and fall of Chinese history. The Great Wall is not only a test of Chinese endurance and tenacity, but also symbolizes the spirit and strength of the Chinese people and is far more than just the greatest engineering project on the planet. It is an umbilical cord that connects the Chinese people with the universe, glorifying the 5,000 years of Chinese civilization.

In China, everyone knows the saying "He who does not reach the Great Wall is not a true man."

乐山大佛 LESHAN GIANT BUDDHA

Built During the Tang Dynasty (618–907), the Leshan Giant Buddha is the largest stone Buddha statue in the world. It was carved out of a cliff face that lies at the confluence of the Mingjiang, Dadu and Qingyi rivers in the southern part of Sichuan Province, near the city of Leshan. The Giant Buddha, in a sitting posture, faces Mount Emei, with the rivers flowing below his feet.

Construction began in 713, initiated by a monk named Haitong. Hoping that the Giant Buddha would bring the water spirit under control, and calm the turbulent water that had plagued numerous shipping vessels travelling down the rivers, Haitong had begged alms for 20 years, and finally accumulated enough money for the project. The project was half finished when Haitong passed away. Two of his disciples continued the work until it was completed in 803, after 90 years of hardship and the efforts of thousands of craftsmen and workers. The massive construction resulted in the removal of stone from the cliff face and this was deposited into the rivers below, thus facilitating navigation on them.

At 233ft (71m) tall, the statue depicts a seated Maitreya Buddha with his hands resting on his knees. The 26ft (8m) long instep is big enough for a hundred people to sit on and each of the 92ft (28m) wide shoulder is large enough for a basketball playground. There is a local saying "The mountain is a Buddha and the Buddha is a mountain."

The charm of the Giant Buddha lies not only in its size, but also in its architecture. There are 1,021 buns skillfully embedded in the Buddha's coiled hair. The drainage system, which helps displace rainwater and keep the inner part of the statue dry, is made up of hidden gutters and channels on the head and arms and behind the ears and in the clothes. It prevents erosion and weathering. The large pair of ears, as well as the nose, are made of wood and are decorated by mud on the surface, which was a magic difficulty for craftsmen more than one thousand years ago.

The nearby Mount Emei is called the "Mountain of Brightness"and it is one of the four famous sacred mountains of Buddhism in China. The area of Mount Emei is one of the places where Buddhism first became established in China, and it is also a religious centre for Taoists throughout history.

In 1996, Mount Emei and the Leshan Giant Buddha were collectively designated a UNESCO World Heritage site.

敦煌莫高窟 MOGAO CAVES IN DUNHUANG

DUNHUANG, a small city in Gansu Province, has for centuries lain on the cultural and religious crossroads between Central Asia and China. A major stop along the Silk Road, it had been a trading post since the 1st century BC. It grew in importance when Emperor Wu of the Han Dynasty (206 BC–220 AD) began to expand the Chinese empire westwards. This was an area where many ethnicities lived together, including the Han, Mongol, Uighur, Tibetan and Hsia peoples.

Since the early centuries of their religion, Buddhist monks from Central Asia had spread their knowledge and interpretations of the scriptures by way of the Silk Road. As an important station on the route, Dunhuang became the stop where foreign monks learned the Chinese language and culture before entering central China. It was here that some of the earliest Buddhist communities in China were formed. Dunhuang also became a centre of Buddhist translation. Enormous economic and human resources were devoted to the production of sutras and scriptures and to the building of places of worship, including Dunhuang's famed grottoes. By the 5th century, Dunhuang had become one of the most important centres of Buddhism along the Silk Road.

The Mogao Caves, also known as the Thousand Buddhas Caves, were carved out of the bluffs stretching 5,250ft (1,600m) along the eastern side of Mingsha Hill, 25km southeast of Dunhuang. With a total of 492 caves, covered by 54,000 square yards (45,000sq.m) of frescoes and containing over two thousand painted statues, the Mogao Caves probably make up the world's most extraordinary gallery of Buddhist art — a gallery whose magnificent murals and stucco sculptures were not collected from distant sources, but created by monks and disciples over the course of nearly a thousand years. The written documents, silk paintings and woodblock prints preserved in the caves reveal contact with virtually every major Buddhist centre in Central Asia and throughout the Chinese empire.

According to legend, the monk Lezun founded the Mogao Caves in 366 AD after having a holy vision. One evening, as the last rays of the sun struck the peak of the mountain, Lezun gazed up to see the Maitreya Buddha bathed in a golden light, surrounded by a host of celestial maidens playing musical instruments and dancing for his entertainment. Awe-struck, Lezun immediately took up hammer and chisel, hollowed out the first of the grottoes and painted his vision there.

The number of grottoes eventually grew to more than a thousand. Artistic representations from the Jin Dynasty (265–420) through the Yuan Dynasty (1206–1368) can be found here, completed through the centuries by both Dunhuang's Buddhist monks and itinerant pilgrims. The grottoes served as hermitages and temples. The paintings and structures served as aids to meditation, as visual representations of the quest for enlightenment, as mnemonic devices, and as teachings for the illiterate populace. Today, the Mogao Caves remain the best example of Buddhist cave art found in China. The Mogao Caves are listed as one of the UNESCO World Heritage sites, and some precious items from them are now exhibits at the British Museum.

Wall painting in the Mogao Grottoes, Dunhuang

丽江古城 OLD TOWN OF LIJIANG

THE OLD TOWN OF LIJIANG is located in the northwest of Yunnan Province, which is blessed with beautiful scenery. Once a confluence for trade along the old tea-horse road, the town has a history of more than a thousand years. Built by the ancestors of the Naxi ethnic people during the 12th and 13th centuries and surrounded by mountains, it combines history, culture and the beauty of nature.

The town is famous for its simple and unique layout. Ancient Chinese towns usually adopted a pattern of rectangular street-alley grids with surrounding formidable high walls. The old town of Lijiang, instead, extends in all directions with the Sifang square street as its centre. The town has an ingenious network of waterways. Shielded by high mountains on three sides, the town is irrigated by three fast-flowing canals, forming an extraordinary landscape of watercourses with houses along their banks. The water arteries of the old town, together with a backdrop of a unique Naxi architecture, present a serene and romantic picture with vibrant colour.

Lijiang boasts the unique Naxi culture. The Naxi people descended from Tibetan nomads and they have a matriarchal family tradition and a unique script that has lasted for more than a thousand years. This script consists of pictograms and is kept alive by some learned individuals. Sometimes you can see old Naxi men playing traditional Chinese music on antique instruments. Called the Dongba culture, the traditional culture of the Naxi people is based on the Dongba religion. Believers practice witchcraft and are skilled in medicine, and transmit their culture through literature and art.

Lijiang is also the home of murals painted during the Ming Dynasty (1368–1644). They cover a total area of 166.5 square yards (139.22sq.m) on 55 walls in Dabaoji Palace, Liuli Hall, Dabao Pavilion and Daque Palace in Baisha. The largest contains 600 figures.

A UNESCO World Heritage site, the old town of Lijiang is one of the last surviving ancient towns in China. It presents a harmonious fusion of different cultural traditions. Snow-capped mountains, cobbled streets, bridges and houses, canals and waterways, as well as the people and their distinct culture, grant Lijiang its universal value to mankind.

布达拉宫 POTALA PALACE

POTALA PALACE is the world's "highest" palace, at an altitude of 12,323ft (3,756m), where it sits in splendour atop Marpo Ri Hill in the northwest of the city of Lhasa. In 1994, it was added to the UNESCO World Heritage list.

The palace was first built in 637 by King Songtsen Gampo for his bride Princess Wen Cheng of the Tang Dynasty. Unfortunately, most of the original building was destroyed by weathering and warfare. When reconstruction started in 1645 (during the Qing Dynasty), the project lasted for nearly half a century. Since then, the Potala Palace was the religious and political centre of Tibet before it was converted into a museum in the second half of the twentieth century.

The Potala Palace consists of two major parts — the Red Palace and the White Palace — and is built mainly of wood and granite. In total the palace is about 384ft (117m) tall and has a floor area of over 5 square miles (13sq.km).

The Red Palace is the central block of the complex and a sacred place for Buddhist prayer and study. It houses the sacred towers of eight Dalai Lamas (in Buddhism, towers are used to house deceased monks), and there are many chapels, shrines, sacred statues and libraries for Buddhist studies. The Red Palace is distinguished from the rest of the palace by its crimson and gilt canopies.

The Sacred Tower of the Fifth Dalai Lama, the biggest of the eight towers, is 49ft (14.85m) tall and is decorated with gold, jewellery and other treasures; it also contains the holy sarira of Buddha and many other priceless antiques. The Great West Hall beside the tower is the biggest in the Potala Palace and famous for its murals that illustrate events in the fifth Dalai Lama's life, including his meeting with Emperor Shun Zhi in Beijing in 1652.

The White Palace comprises the east wing of the Potala Palace. In the past it used to serve as the seat of the local government of Tibet and also the main residence of the Dalai Lama. It contains living quarters, offices, the seminary and the printing house. The western block of the Palace is for ordinary lamas and, due to its white walls, it is often considered part of the White Palace.

Today the Potala Palace has become a great museum for learning the history and culture of Tibet, China. Its grand layout and unique design make it one of the greatest architectural wonders of the world, and it remains a holy site for Buddhists.

澳门大三巴 RUINS OF ST. PAUL'S, MACAO

MACAO, the bustling, neon-lit port city in south China also known as the "Vegas of the East", has long stood at the confluence of East and West. Portugese settlers first arrived here in 1513, followed by Jesuit missionaries, who founded St. Paul's Cathedral in 1580. The remnant facade of the structure provides unique testimony to a bygone place and era when Catholicism first spread in China.

St. Paul's was the first Western-style building in Macao, featuring a white stone facade, a majestic vaulted roof and elaborately decorated halls. It twice caught fire, in 1595 and 1601, and was reconstructed in 1637. At one time it was the largest Catholic church in all of Asia, and was home to St. Paul's College, the first Western college in East Asia. In 1835, both cathedral and college were destroyed by fire, leaving only the baroque facade which one finds today, and the crypts of their Jesuit founders.

Today, the ruins of St. Paul's stand above a small hill, with sixty-six steps leading up to the entrance. The facade of the former cathedral is adorned by numerous statues and carvings, meticulously rendered by local artisans and exiled Japanese Christians, under the guidance of the Jesuit missionary Carlo Spinola (1564–1622).

The subjects of the sculptures range from Chinese lions and Japanese chrysanthemums to founders of the Jesuit Order and mythological figures. These include the striking figure of a woman trampling on a seven-headed hydra, the serpentine beast of Greek mythology, described in Chinese as "the Holy Mother trampling on the heads of a dragon".

In the 1990s, with the excavation of the crypts, numerous religious artefacts and relics were discovered at the site. Among them are the relics of Japanese Christian martyrs, believed to have arrived in Macao fleeing persecution by the Japanese bakufu. Also here is the tomb of Father Alessandro Valignano, founder of St. Paul's College.

In the two centuries in which

St. Paul's Cathedral stood erect on the hill, the Jesuits left a lasting influence in China. Among the luminaries associated with St. Paul's College are the German-born Johann Adam Schall von Bell (1591–1666), who served in the imperial court, and the great missionary and scholar Matteo Ricci (1552–1610). The Jesuit-founded St. Raphael's Hospital, currently home to the Portugese consulate in Macao, helped to introduce Western medicine to China, and pioneered the use of the smallpox vaccine.

The ruined St. Paul's, now a museum, is the most famous landmark in Macao. In 2005, it was included as part of the "Historic Centre of Macao", designated UNESCO World Heritage status.

哈尼梯田 TERRACED FIELDS OF HANI

Between the Red River and the Lancang River, in the mountains of southwest China, vast, terraced fields wind from one mountain to another. Over generations, some 31 square miles (80sq.km) of hill slopes have been carved into terraces, transforming a barren valley into fertile fields of rice crops. The stair-like, seemingly never-ending rice fields have been cultivated by the Hani people for at least 1,300 years, and remain in use today. They are claimed to be the world's most spectacular terraced fields.

The terraced fields are located in the town of Yuanyang in Yunnan Province, a Hani minority settlement on the Ailao mountain range at an elevation of about 5,150ft (1,570m). The Hani people are possibly the earliest rice farmers in China. From generation to generation, their lives are interwoven with the rice paddies. A new-born Hani baby cannot have a formal name until a ritual in the terraced fields is performed for him. After death, the Hani people are buried on the hillsides near the fields.

The terraced fields are adapted to the high altitude, the climate and the steep slopes of the hills. Water evaporates from the fields to form clouds; the clouds give rain, which is trapped and gathered by the forests on the mountains. Then, water from the mountain springs flows down to the terraced fields, and the entire cycle repeats itself. From winter to early spring, the fields are irrigated with spring water from the forest above to be rejuvenated and prepared for the next growing season.

The fields, which are flooded from December to April, create a reflecting pool effect, attracting photographers from all over the world. In summer, the fields are luxuriantly green with growing rice stalks. After the autumn harvest, they become bare earth.

天安门 TIAN'ANMEN

HAVE YOU EVER been to Beijing, the capital of China? If so, you must have been to Tian'anmen Square in the centre of the city. If you see a photo of a large portrait of Mao Zedong, the first Chairman of the People's Republic of China, hung on a castle-size building, you have found a picture of the Tian'anmen Tower, after which the square is named.

The Tian'anmen Tower is probably equivalent in stature to the White House in the USA, but it is not a residence or an office. It was part of the City Wall surrounding the Forbidden City, which used to house the imperial court. The Forbidden City was built during the Ming Dynasty (1368–1644), shortly after the Emperor Zhu established Beijing as the capital. Tian'anmen was called Chengtian Gate at that time. Located in the middle section of the southern wall, Chengtian Gate guarded the entrance to the Forbidden City. The name was changed in the Qing Dynasty (1616–1911) to the present name, "Tian'anmen".

The layout of the Forbidden City was largely symmetrical. A number of other gates were built to the north and south of Tian'anmen, and the City Ring was connected to the Suburb Ring south of Tian'anmen, leaving room for market fairs and traffic. Tian'anmen and vicinity gained prominence through repeated expansions during the Qing Dynasty, with new towers and side gates built around the square. Unfortunately, none of them survived the urbanization during the Republic of China years (1912–1949).

Today, visitors can tour various museums located in the vicinity of Tian'anmen Square. Occupying 109 acres (44 hectares), Tian'anmen Square is the largest open urban square in the world. The Tower is the historical site of Chairman Mao's inauguration in 1949. The red lanterns that have decorated this building since then were designed by two Japanese artists who had come to China in the 1930s to join in the building of a new China. The mural of Chairman Mao, 20ft (6m) by 16ft (5m) in size, is currently in its fourth edition, and looks over the square from the south-facing wall of the Tian'anmen Tower. The current version was painted by Ge Xiaoguang.

Monument to the People's Heroes

福建土楼 TULOUS

THE TULOUS ARE THE unique earthen dwellings of the Hakka and other peoples in the mountainous areas of southwestern Fujian Province. Built between the 12th and 20th centuries, these immense rammed-earth structures have a fortress-like appearance, either circular or rectangular in shape, with one main entrance guarded by thick wooden doors, and small windows on the upper levels of the compound. Housing up to several dozen families at a time, the tulous are extraordinary representations of unique communities whose members are bound not only by blood lineage but also in common defence against a potentially hostile environment. In parts of Fujian, the tulous continue to be inhabited, and a number of them have become accessible to tourists.

Take a glance at the local histories of southeastern China and you will find that the region was plagued by armed banditry and skirmishes. In the remote areas of Fujian Province, the early settlers built mountaintop strongholds, which evolved into the complete fortified tulous. The tulous have thick outer walls virtually immune to arrows and gunfire, with the lower sections built from granite blocks or large river cobbles. With their smaller ends pointing outwards, any effort to dislodge the cobbles from the outside is futile. The upper parts of the walls are built from rammed earth and a mixture of lime, sand and clay, reinforced laterally with bamboo or wooden strips. Even cannon-fire would only make a small dent on these walls.

Each tulou compound has one main entrance, especially designed for defense. The double doors, with the frame made of large, solid granite beams, are reinforced with thick iron plates. In order to prevent fire, some gates are equipped with water tanks at the top. From gunholes at the top of the building, the inhabitants are able to fire at enemies outside.

The tulous are not only remarkable fortresses but extraordinary structures for communal living. With the number of rooms ranging from several to nearly three hundred, they house anywhere from a family clan of several generations to an entire village community. The rooms are identical — of the same size, built from the same material, and decorated in similar fashion. Rooms at the ground level are used as kitchens and dining rooms. Those on the second floor are used for storage. Rooms on the third and fourth floors are used as bedrooms. Smaller families occupied one vertical set of rooms from the ground level to the third or fourth floor, while larger families owned two or three vertical sets.

All branches of the clan shared the same roof, symbolizing unity. All the rooms face the ancestral hall at the centre of the compound on the ground level. In the grounds there are many other communal facilities — water wells, the outhouse, wash rooms, weaponry, and even farmland and orchards.

The Hakka people are generally said to have built the tulous, but the origin of these unique structures remains controversial. Solid as castles and technologically sophisticated, they are regarded as exceptional examples of a flourishing tradition in which communal living is integrated harmoniously with the environment.

Internal and external views of a tulou

129

大雁塔 WILD GOOSE PAGODA

THE WILD GOOSE PAGODA, in Xi'an, Shanxi Province, was built during the early Tang Dynasty (618–907). It housed the sutras and relics of the Buddha brought back from India by the great Buddhist hierarch Xuanzang (602–664). The original structure was built as part of the Da Ci'en Temple (Great Compassion Temple) in 589. Li Zhi, who later became the Emperor Gaozong (reigned 649–683), rebuilt the temple in memory of his mother, who suffered an early death.

During the Tang Dynasty, Da Ci'en Temple was located inside a walled compound in the southeastern sector of the capital city of Chang'an (present-day Xi'an). Departing from Chang'an, the monk Xuanzang travelled along the Silk Road to the Buddhist holy land of India, and amassed a substantial collection of sutras and figurines during his 17 years on the road. After returning to Chang'an, Xuanzang became the first abbot of Da Ci'en Temple and supervised the building of the Wild Goose Pagoda. With the support of the imperial court, he invited many hierarchs into the temple to translate Sanskrit sutras into Chinese, a total of 1,335 volumes. He also wrote a book entitled *Travel Notes on the Western Regions of the Great Tang*, on which Wu Cheng'en, a novelist of the Ming Dynasty (1368–1644), based his famed opus *Pilgrimage to the West* many centuries later.

At the time of its completion in 652, the Wild Goose Pagoda stood five stories high, with a stone exterior encasing an interior layer of rammed earth. The structure collapsed five decades later, and the Empress Wu Zetian (reigned 690–705) had the pagoda rebuilt, adding five more stories. The current construction, whose facade dates from the Ming Dynasty (1368–1644), stands seven stories high.

An architectural marvel, the pagoda was built with layers of bricks without cement in between. The Buddha is depicted on the doorframes and the four sides of the base. The vivid shapes and smooth lines of the stone sculptures reveal supreme craftsmanship.

During the Tang Dynasty, successful candidates who passed the imperial examinations would ascend the pagoda to inscribe writings and poems. The custom was passed down through the centuries to the Ming dynasty.

As the oldest extant structure in present-day Xi'an, the Wild Goose Pagoda serves as a witness to the prosperity of the Tang Dynasty and the widespread influence of Buddhist culture at the time. It is regarded as a landmark of Xi'an.

Left: The Wild Goose Pagoda
Below: Statue with pagoda in the background

4

CEREMONIES &
FESTIVALS

节庆仪式

端午节 DRAGON-BOAT FESTIVAL

THE DRAGON-BOAT FESTIVAL is a traditional Chinese festival, known in Chinese as the "Duanwu Festival". It is associated with the death of the great patriot and poet Qu Yuan (340–278 BC), who was a native of the kingdom of Chu (in present-day Hubei Province) and lived during the Warring States period (475–221 BC).

In history, Qu Yuan was a descendant of the imperial family and served as a high-ranking official in the kingdom of Chu. He warned his king against alliance with the kingdom of Qin, but was accused of treason and exiled from the land. History proved Qu Yuan correct; the kingdom of Qin grew increasingly powerful, conquering a number of neighbouring kingdoms, and eventually turned its back on Chu. When the army of Qin seized Chu's capital, Qu Yuan, hearing of the news in a distant land, was so stricken with sadness that he ended his life by jumping into the Miluo River (located in present-day Hunan Province).

Hearing of their beloved poet's death, the local residents immediately searched for him in the river, rowing hundreds of boats. Concerned that his body would be devoured by fish, they made zongzi (rice stuffed with a variety of fillings and wrapped in bamboo leaves) and threw them into the river to appease the hungry fish. In this way, the traditions of dragon-boat racing and eating zongzi on this day were born.

The dragon-boat race, held annually on the day of Qu Yuan's death, has since evolved into a joyous event. What makes it unique is the size of the boat — the average length is about 66ft (20m), and larger boats can be over 98ft (30m) long, seating more than 50 rowers. The head of a dragon is fixed at the front of the boat and its tail at the end. Dragon scales are painted or engraved on the side of the boat, so that it is really a spectacular sight when the race takes place, appearing like a dragon ready to take off from the surface of the water.

Zongzi has also grown popular throughout China, with many regional variations. In the southern province of Guangxi, zongzi comes in enormous sizes, stuffed with meat and weighing up to 2 pounds (900g). Smaller varieties are found in Shanghai and its vicinity — as tiny as a one-inch long nibble.

Left: A dragon-boat race; Above: Zongzi

元宵节 LANTERN FESTIVAL

Yuanxiao (glutinous rice balls)

EVERY YEAR, on the fifteenth day of the first lunar month, the Chinese celebrate the Lantern Festival by eating yuanxiao (glutinous rice balls), watching lanterns, and setting off fireworks at night. In Chinese, the festival is called the Yuanxiao Festival, as the first lunar month is the "yuan" month and "xiao" means "night". The festival marks the end of the Spring Festival celebrations, and is sometimes also known as the Minor Spring Festival. Held on the first full-moon night of the lunar new year, it is associated with harmony and togetherness.

The highlight of the celebrations takes place at night, when lanterns of various colours, shapes and sizes illuminate the streets. Many buildings are decorated with lanterns, outlining their silhouettes and presenting views of real grandeur. The lanterns often depict auspicious images and words. Children go out on the streets carrying small lanterns, usually in the shape of animals. The whole scene appears brilliant, and the aura dreamlike.

An indispensable part of the Lantern Festival is yuanxiao (also called tangyuan in southern China), whose round shape symbolizes reunion. Glutinous rice flour is mixed with water to produce the dough, which is then made into round little balls in the palm. Plain yuanxiao consists of only dough, but it is much more delicious with fillings. Sesame paste is the most common filling; other popular choices include bean paste, peanuts, chopped vegetables and meat. While yuanxiao is usually served boiled, it can also be steamed or fried.

Celebrations revolving around the first full moon of the new year date back two millenia. According to *Records of the Grand Historian*, emperors of the Han Dynasty (206 BC–220 AD) held splendid ceremonies on this day to pray to Taiyi, the God of Heaven, for good weather and fortune. Later, with the introduction of Buddhism to China, lanterns were lit in reverence to the Buddha. The Lantern Festival is also said to celebrate the birth of Tianguan, one of the three Emperors of Heaven in the Taoist tradition. By the Tang Dynasty (618–907), the festival had evolved into a national carnival, with curfew lifted for three days to allow for revelry.

Today, the Lantern Festival remains a joyous and important day. In almost every city and town, there is a designated place for lantern displays. The streets are crowded with excited viewers, who wander in search of the best-designed lanterns. Performances such as lion dances, magic tricks, puppet shows, aerobatics and folk theatre are held everywhere. Among the festival's popular diversions is guessing answers to riddles posted on the lanterns. The riddles often convey messages about fortune, harvest and health. Usually everyone can have a try, and the winners are awarded small prizes.

中秋节 MID-AUTUMN FESTIVAL

FALLING ON THE 15TH of the eighth lunar month (usually around mid- or late September in the Gregorian calendar), the Mid-Autumn Festival (also known as the "Moon Festival") is regarded primarily as an occasion for members of a family (often an extended one) to get together because ancient Chinese believed that on the night of the 15th or 16th of the eighth lunar month the moon was at its roundest and brightest, symbolizing family union. It has always been one of the three most important traditional holidays in China (the other two being the Dragon-Boat Festival and the Spring Festival) and was given the statutory status of a public holiday by the Chinese legislature in 2008.

The custom of celebrating the Mid-Autumn Festival has two alleged origins. The first one, dated back to the Zhou Dynasty (c. 1029–256 BC), was ancient Chinese moon worship, which features sacrifice-making to the full moon on the night of the mid-autumn day to pray for good harvests, health and longevity, conjugal bliss, and family solidarity. Another one was the legend of Lady Chang'E, the Chinese Goddess of the Moon, which began to spread in China at the end of the Warring States Period (475–221 BC). According to the legend, Lady Chang'E ate the drug of immortality her husband Houyi entrusted to her and was lifted up to the sky under the magical power of the drug and made to live forever in the chilly Moon Palace, away from her husband. Folk had great sympathy for the lonely Chang'E (now their Moon Goddess of Immortality), so they made sacrifices to the moon on this day of the year when the moon displays the largest illuminated area, expressing their wish for her return to the human world. By the end of the Tang Dynasty (618–907), the tradition of observing the festival had been firmly established, as evidenced in the numerous romantic poems Tang poets composed to delineate scenes of enjoying moonlight and moon cakes on this day, and to celebrate the loveliness of Lady Chang'E. In the Song Dynasty (960–1279), the court declared the 15th day of the eighth lunar month to be the Mid-Autumn Festival.

A number of folk customs are associated with this festival, the most popular one being sharing moon cakes with one's nearest and dearest while appreciating the beautiful view of a full moon shining in the heavens and enjoying its pleasant, soothing beam. Other customs include collecting dandelion leaves and distributing them among family members, burning incense in reverence to deities (including Goddess Chang'E), offering moon cakes as gifts to friends and neighbours, (for children) putting pomelo rinds on one's head, walking around with brightly lit lanterns, rowing a boat in the moonlight, staging dragon dances, etc.

Most familiar sacrifices offered to the moon on the night of the Mid-Autumn Festival are taro roots, pomegranates, pomelo, wine fermented with the flowers of sweet osmanthus (*Osmanthus fragrans*) and of course, the indispensible, exclusive holiday token moon cakes. A moon cake is an exquisitely made round cake, filled with preserved fruits, nuts, sweetened bean paste, sugar syrup, meat, etc. The round shape it takes symbolizes union or consummation. The prototype of the present-day moon cakes was said to be the round flat cakes which Li Yuan (566–635), the first emperor of the Tang Dynasty, received from a Turfan businessman as a tribute and which he shared with his subjects (hence the tradition of sharing moon cakes among family members and friends).

Due to the influence of Chinese culture, the Mid-Autumn Festival is also observed in some other Asian countries.

Left: Appreciating the full moon
Right: Moon cakes

七夕节 NIGHT OF SEVENS FESTIVAL

Niulang, the cowherd, meeting Zhinü, the weaving girl, across the Milky Way

A Chinese hanging scroll (10th century), Palace Banquet, in the Metropolitan Museum of Art, shows the cerebration of this festival

ALSO KNOWN as the "Women's Festival to Plead for Skills" or the "Seventh Sister's Birthday", the Night of Sevens Festival is a traditional Chinese holiday to celebrate the yearly reunion of a young married couple who had been forcibly separated. It falls on the seventh night of the seventh month in the Chinese lunisolar calendar, hence its name, which literally means the "Seventh Night of the Seventh Month Festival". In the Gregorian calendar, it is a movable night in August.

In ancient Chinese legend, the stars Altair and Vega were a loving couple named Niulang ("Cowherd") and Zhinü ("Weaving Girl"). The Milky Way, instead of being a royal path leading to the palace of Zeus or the milk sprayed from Hera's breasts, as described in Greek fables, is a vast river that lies between Niulang and Zhinü and prevents them from meeting each other.

The legend about the two stars has been kept alive for over two millennia in China. Its prototype dates back to as early as the Warring States period (475–221 BC). The most widely circulated version has it that once upon a time there was a poor, kindhearted orphan boy named Niulang. The boy's mean elder brother and sister-in-law gave him a cow and drove him out of their home. One day Niulang encountered seven fairies bathing in a lake. The youngest, or the seventh, of them, Zhinü, was a granddaughter of the Jade Emperor of Heaven and his wife the Queen Mother of the West. Before she sneaked out of Heaven to relax for a while in the mortal world, she had been busily engaged in weaving rosy clouds every day with which her grandmother decorated the sky. She fell in love with Niulang, so instead of returning to Heaven with her sisters, she stayed behind and married the cowherd. The couple led a happy life and bore two children.

The Queen Mother of the West, however, was infuriated with her granddaughter's marrying a mere mortal and decided to take her back to Heaven. When Niulang found that his beloved wife had been abducted by the Queen Mother of the West, he was shocked. Shouldering his two kids in two wicker baskets, he ran after them. Just as he was about to catch up with his wife, however, the Queen Mother of the West took off a hairpin from her head and waved it across the sky. A rushing river (the Milky Way) immediately appeared in front of Niulang, separating the couple forever. Since then, Zhinü has been sitting at her loom day by day, sadly weaving for her grandmother, while Niulang can only watch her from the other side of the river while taking care of their children. However, the couple have remained faithful to each other all the time, which moved even magpies. Every year, on the night of the seventh of the seventh month, magpies all over the world would fly up the sky to form a bridge across the Milky Way so that Niulang and Zhinü could reunite with each other on it, although only for no more than one night.

An important holiday in China for many centuries, the Night of Sevens is still widely observed in rural China. On that day, single or newly married women are expected to present fruits, incense, etc. to Zhinü as offerings in order that they may be blessed with good skills in needlecraft as well as a happy marriage. In recent years, some young people in urban areas have tried to revitalize this age-old festival and celebrated it as one of the two Chinese Valentine's Days (the other being the Lantern Festival).

The influence of the Night of Sevens Festival can be felt in some other Asian countries, too. In Korea, Vietnam, and Japan, for example, there are similar stories about the Night of Sevens although the names of the hero and heroine differ slightly from those in the Chinese original.

Offering sacrifices at graves

清明节 QINGMING FESTIVAL

ANCESTOR WORSHIP, an important element of traditional Chinese culture, is anchored in the belief that one's deceased ancestors still inhabit this world — even if in another dimension or space. They still need housing, food and money, and they are continually in touch with the world of posterity. Unsurprisingly, a special festival is observed in memory of the ancestors, when offerings are given and prayers exchanged. This day is known as the Qingming Festival, and has been observed for over 2,000 years.

The Qingming Festival falls on the 15th day after the vernal equinox, typically between April 4th and 6th. It marks the fifth of the twenty-four Solar Terms in the traditional Chinese calendar. "Qingming" literally means "clear and bright", though the changing of the seasons often indicates rain. According to one proverb, "for sowing and planting, the best time is Qingming". In this regard,

Qingming is an important time for agricultural activities.

Yet as a festival, Qingming is much more than merely a weather marker. Across the country, people remember and honour their departed kin on this day. At the graves of the deceased, sacrifices including food and wine are offered, along with funerary money, which is burned in front of the tomb. It is believed that this imitation paper money is the currency of the underworld, received when it is burnt. Sometimes, small paper houses small paper furniture or even paper horses are "sent" to the deceased in this way. Some people kowtow to the graves of their forebears, expressing veneration and praying to them for good luck and protection. This special day is a family occasion. Members of large extended families, sometimes tracing back for four or more generations, gather in reverence to their common, deceased kin.

While the Qingming Festival may seem a somber occasion, it also has a lively aspect. People enjoy being outdoors, picnicking, flying kites and playing on the swings. A popular custom is planting willow branches around the house; children weave the branches into wreaths and wear them on their heads. It is said that willows help divert bad luck and disease, and that, like willows, which grow easily and vigorously wherever they are planted, family members are blessed to prosper wherever they go.

春节 SPRING FESTIVAL

FROM A SECULAR PERSPECTIVE, what the Spring Festival is to the Chinese is quite the same as what Christmas is to people in the West. Traditionally a holiday to mark the passing of the old year and the arrival of the new, and to make offerings to gods and ancestors, the Spring Festival (also known as the "Chinese New Year") is nowadays mainly a season for family reunions. It is the single most important public as well as traditional holiday in China and one of the major holidays in other Asian countries with a sizable Chinese population, including Burma, Korea, Indonesia, Malaysia, Singapore, Thailand and Vietnam. On this holiday, people staying away from home and members of an extended family would try their best to get back to join their parents, spouses, and children, and family members would meet and stay together for a relatively long period of time.

The Spring Festival has its origin in the ancient Chinese legend of "Nian" (literally "Year" in Chinese), a mystical beast that allegedly came to villages on the first day of the year to devour livestock, crops and even children. At first, villagers were frightened when Nian appeared, but later they found that the sound of burning wood could scare the beast away. In the year that followed, people made firecrackers and let them off when Nian came to assault them. Nian was scared away and never dared to show up again. From then on, people would celebrate the successful exorcizing of Nian at the beginning of each lunar year and the term "guonian" (literally, "passing the year") began to be used to refer to New Year celebrations.

It has been discovered that the lunar New Year was celebrated by the Chinese as early as the Xia Dynasty (ca. 2070–1600 BC), but it was not until the Han Dynasty (206 BC–220 AD) that the first lunar month was finally established as the beginning of a year and the first day of that month regarded as the formal beginning of the Spring Festival. In the Gregorian calendar, the Spring Festival falls on a movable date between January 21st and February 20th.

Purchasing decorations for Spring Festival

As a statutory public holiday in present-day China, the Spring Festival starts on the last day of the twelfth lunar month and lasts for seven days (including a weekend). In the folk tradition, however, the Festival begins much earlier and lasts longer, usually from the 8th of the twelfth lunar month to the 15th of the first lunar month.

The 8th day of the twelfth lunar month is called "Laba" (the Eighth of the Twelfth Lunar Month) because the twelfth month in a lunar year is known as "Layue" (the Twelfth Lunar Month) in Chinese. On that day, people, monasteries and (in imperial years) the court would cook "Laba congee", a kind of mixed congee, to offer to Buddha as sacrifice, to give to Buddhist monks, nuns and court officials as gifts, to hand out to the poor as charity food as well as to share among family members.

The 23rd or 24th day is the "Minor Lunar New Year Day" of the entire holiday season. It is a time for people to cook appetizing dishes for the Kitchen God, who is supposed to have been sent by the Jade Emperor of Heaven to monitor and record the functioning of each household, and who is to leave for heaven on this day to report to his lord on the household's good deeds and transgressions in the past year. (Nowadays, people make or buy delicious food on this day more to treat themselves than to give the Kitchen God a pleasing send-off.)

Touching off the firecracker

The 28th day is typically associated with washing, sweeping and mopping. People give their houses a thorough clean-up so that bad luck will be left back in the old year. After the 28th, people refrain from sweeping the floor, believing that sweeping may drive away the family's good fortune in the coming new year.

The year-end household clean-up is usually followed by the adorning of the house with festive decorations. The most familiar ornament on the door is Spring Festival couplets, or auspicious antithetic sentences written vertically on two narrow pieces of red paper using a Chinese writing brush. Usually pasted on the door panels, the couplets express people's wishes for peace, good harvest, family prosperity, etc. in the new year. Windows are also decorated, usually with "window flowers" — paper cutouts pasted on window panes that feature graceful patterns of flowers and animals or auspicious Chinese characters.

The most important time of the holiday season is New Year's Eve, when family members sit around the table and enjoy a very sumptuous dinner known as "family reunion dinner" or "New Year's Eve dinner". A person spending Spring Festival in China for the first time would be amazed at the sheer quantity and variety of the food prepared for this special occasion. An indispensable course of the dinner is fish, which, however, is not to be consumed completely. That is a gesture with the symbolic meaning of "may there be surpluses (fish) every year", as in Chinese "fish" and "surplus" share the same pronunciation "yu". After the dinner, people in the north make jiaozi (a kind of dumpling) and have them after midnight. Jiaozi resemble gold ingots in shape, so eating them is also a symbolic expression of the wish for wealth in the new year. People in the south make niangao (New Year cake, a kind of ground rice cake) and send them as gifts to neighbours and relatives in the next few days as a token of their good wishes, because in Chinese "gao" (cake) and "gao" (high) have the same pronunciation and "niangao" is interpreted as meaning "to become increasingly prosperous with each passing year".

On the morning of the first day of the first lunar month, or lunar New Year Day, people rise early to let off fireworks. Setting off firecrackers is an important part of the Chinese New Year celebrations, as people believe that the cracking and popping sounds of firecrackers will drive away evil spirits and ward off bad luck.

The first few days of the New Year are usually spent in visiting relatives, friends and colleagues, and adults will bless their own unmarried children and grandchildren as well as children of other families by giving them yasui qian (literally, "money for suppressing evil spirits") or red packet, which is a moderate sum of gift money wrapped in red envelopes.

The next important festive occasion falls on the 5th day of the first lunar month, which is alleged to be the birthday of the God of Wealth. On the morning of that day, people let off long strings of firecrackers to welcome the God of Wealth, believing that the more firecrackers they let off, the more wealth they will receive in the new year.

Traditionally, the Spring Festival season ends on the 15th day of the first lunar month with the celebration of the Lantern Festival, when people stage lantern shows and make lantern parades to celebrate the first full moon in the lunar new year. Because it is customary to eat yuanxiao made of ground glutinous rice on that day, the Lantern Festival is also called Yuanxiao Festival in Chinese.

拜堂　WEDDING BOWS

WEDDING BOWS lie at the centre of the traditional Chinese wedding. The ritualistic bows are intended to pay homage to heaven and earth, express gratitude to the older generation, and avow faithfulness between bride and groom.

The bows typically take place on the morning of the wedding day. The groom's family prepare the family altar in advance, placing on it tablets engraved with the names of forebears. Also on the altar are candles, incense burners and offerings such as grains, peanuts and dates.

The bride is carried to the home of the groom in a nuptial sedan chair from the home of her parents. Upon her arrival, firecrackers are set off and the new couple is conducted to the altar. The groom stands on the left side of the altar, and the bride on the right.

When it is time for the wedding bows, two masters of ceremony announce the commands: "Kneel down", "Kowtow", and "Rise", repeated three times. The new couple thus perform their bows. The first bow — kowtow — is to Heaven and Earth. The couple places lit incense in the incense burner, and kowtows to the open space facing the entrance to the room. The second bow is to the the groom's parents; the couple then offer them each a cup of tea. At last, bride and groom kowtow to each other. This completes the ritual and they are then escorted into the nuptial chamber.

In the past, it was only after the three bows that marriage became official. In modern Chinese wedding ceremonies, the bride and bridegroom still perform these bows, but instead of kowtowing they usually just bow deeply.

Bride and bridegroom at a Chinese weddding, ready to bow

抓周 ZHUAZHOU CEREMONY

"ZHUAZHOU", literally "one-year-old catch", is one of the most popular traditional customs in a child's first birthday celebration. It is believed to reveal the child's inner disposition and future vocation.

At the ceremony, the child is carried to a large rice sieve (or sometimes a small table), which holds a variety of articles: a pen, an ink brush, a knife, a ruler, a coin, an abacus, an accounting book, a cooking utensil, a fruit, a seal, a volume of the classics, a scale, a piece of jewellery, a flower, a small case of rouge, a cookie and a toy, etc. If the child is a girl, a sewing box and a book of embroidery designs are added to the mix. Without any guidance, the child is free to choose what pleases him or her the most.

Each of the items is of symbolic significance: the volume of the classics respresents learning and scholarship; the pen and ink brush, calligraphy and painting; the seal, high office; the abacus and the coin, business and commerce. Thus the child who picks the abacus will be shrewd in business; the baby girl who selects the sewing box or book of designs will have deft fingers. As for rouge, for a girl, it indicates the pursuit of beautiful appearance, while for a boy, it signifies romantic encounters and a disposition for the other sex.

Invitation to the ceremony is extended to the entire family and close friends, who in turn prepare gifts or red envelopes enclosing sums of money, and arrive early in the morning to wish the child well. At lunchtime, noodles, symbolizing longevity, are served at a large table, and it is at this time that the ceremony takes place.

Traditionally, at the ceremony the child is dressed in a garment sewn from rags, pieced together and gathered by the mother from her neighbours. In this way, the garment is believed to gather the well-wishers all around, and ensure a peaceful and supportive growing environment for the child.

A zhuazhou ceremony

5

DAILY LIFE

饮食起居

算盘 ABACUS

THE ABACUS is one of the oldest instruments of computation in Asia. Used by the Chinese since ancient times, it remains in living use today.

A modern abacus basically resembles its 14th-century counterpart, divided by a crossbeam into two decks, and framed by thirteen parallel rods that run through the crossbeam at intervals. There are seven beads strung on each rod, with two above the crossbeam in the upper deck and the other five below the beam in the lower deck.

When moved towards the crossbeam, each bead, also known as a counter, represents a number. A bead in the lower deck of the rightmost column is moved upwards to the crossbeam to represent one. If another lower bead is moved, the two beads stand for two. Meanwhile, each upper deck bead represents an increment of five, and are moved downwards towards the crossbeam. All computation begins in the rightmost column of the abacus and moves left, representing the arrangement of the digits.

The abacus is made from various materials, such as wood, brass, iron and even gold. Traditionally, the golden abacus represents prosperity, and is given as a gift to shopkeepers, though it is seldom used. The image of a man working an abacus can represent either a shrewd merchant or a prosperous clerk.

Today, although the abacus has lost its popularity to electronic calculators and computers in the face of complex computations and large-scale counting, it remains a deft instrument for day-to-day transactions in stores. As a reminder of ancient wisdom, embodying functionality in simplicity, every Chinese pupil in elementary school continues to be taught how to use the abacus.

针灸 ACUPUNCTURE & MOXIBUSTION

ACUPUNCTURE AND MOXIBUSTION therapy is an amazing creation of Chinese culture. In simple terms, acupuncture is the insertion of thin needles into the body at specific points, and moxibustion is the application of burning moxa to certain parts of the body. These two methods, often used together as a therapy, can cure many diseases and maintain good health. As shown by historical records and archaeological excavations, this medical treatment dates back to the Neolithic Age, and is very complicated in both theory and practice.

The theory underlying acupuncture is the belief in an invisible network connecting important organs inside the human body. The network consists of meridians (jing, the stems) and collaterals (luo, small branches) through which energy (qi, pronounced "chee") flows and travels around the body. In ancient Chinese philosophy, qi is the fundamental driving force of the universe and can be divided into two types — yin and yang. The human body is viewed as a small universe, permeated by twelve main meridians, eight minor meridians,

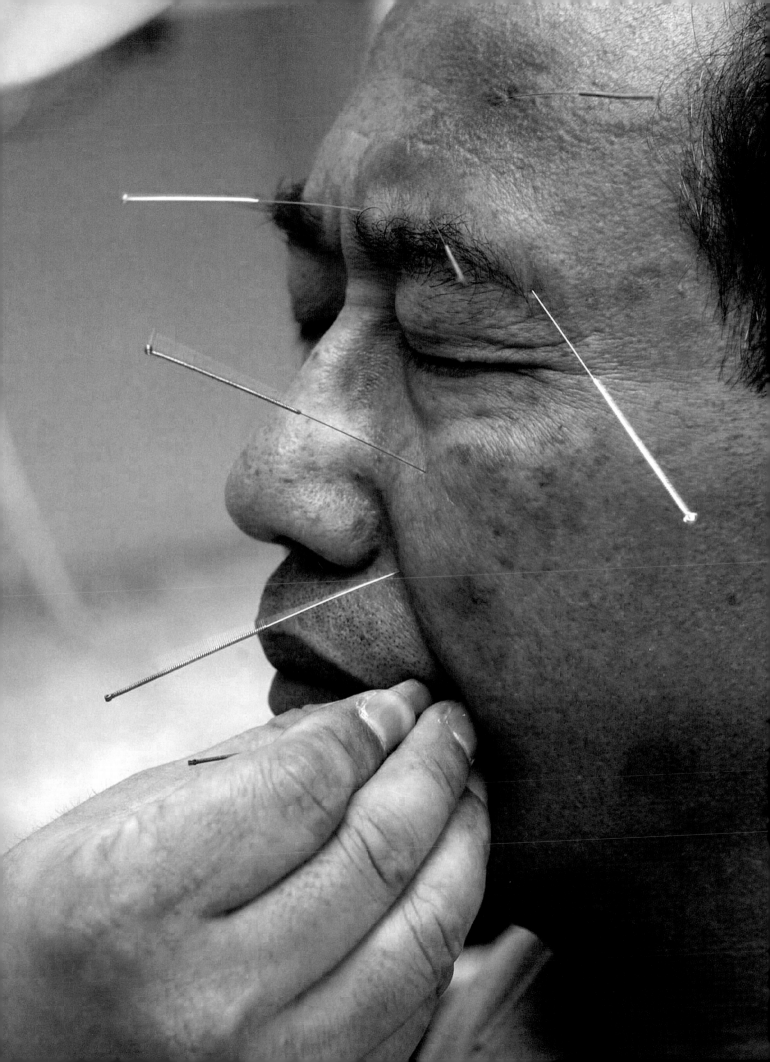

and fifteen collaterals. The body works well when the two types of energy flow smoothly and reach a balance in the organs. If there are blockages or imbalances, symptoms will arise. For example, a blockage of energy in the kidney might cause a problem in the heart, and acupuncture may be used to adjust the energy flow.

Unlike the hollow needles used for injection, acupuncture needles are solid and often made of silver or steel. Different needles, varying in length and diameter, can be chosen to cure different diseases. The doctor may use a number of techniques if necessary. The angle and depth of insertion, as well as the time needed, also depend on the symptoms. A successful acupuncture treatment often causes certain sensations (such as prickling, itching or warmth, as a result of adjusting qi movement) but little pain. In the past, needles were always sterilized by fire, and nowadays disposable needles are used, so you do not have to worry about their hygiene.

In many cases, moxibustion may also be used for better effect, usually as a supplement to acupuncture. The doctor lights moxa (mugwort) and puts it on the skin at certain points. Another way is to attach moxa to the external end of the needle, which will conduct heat into the body. No matter how moxa is used, this treatment is meant to use heat to activate qi and improve the flow of blood.

Acupuncturists sometimes also use cupping to stimulate qi, lighting a small fire in a small jar so as to create a space of lower air pressure or even vacuum. The jar is then placed upside down on the skin so that is adheres to the skin by suction. Cupping causes blood congestion but no pain, and it is very safe if it is performed properly .

As a unique and ingenious creation of traditional Chinese medicine, acupuncture and moxibustion therapy was spread to many other Asian countries including Korea and Japan, as early as in the 6th century. It was introduced to the West in the 17th century, mainly by missionaries. Doubts about it have been fading away while interest continues to grow. In recognition of its safety and efficacy, the World Health Organization recommends acupuncture as the preferred treatment for over forty medical problems. Today many Westerners include this therapy as part of their medical care.

筷子 CHOPSTICKS

CHOPSTICKS ORIGINATED in ancient China at least 3,000 years ago, and they were introduced to other countries, such as Japan and Vietnam, as early as during the Tang Dynasty (618–907). While Westerners use knives and forks at table, the Chinese eat with chopsticks, a pair of thin sticks about 8in (20cm) long. Chopsticks are usually made of bamboo, but they can be made of gold, silver, bronze or jade with colourful patterns painted or carved on the stem. Today, chopsticks remain popular in many Asian countries and are used by an estimated population of more than 1.5 billion people daily.

As a unique eating utensil, chopsticks reveal an important aspect of Chinese culture, showing a preference for balance and co-operation rather than confrontation. Unlike the use of knife and fork, using chopsticks does not involve any cutting or piercing; instead it requires coordinated finger movement. Held between the thumb and fingers of one hand, chopsticks are used like tongs to pick up portions of food that is already prepared and brought to the table in small and convenient pieces. Chopsticks may also be used as means for sweeping rice and other small morsels into the mouth directly from the bowl.

Many rules of etiquette govern the use of chopsticks: they are traditionally held only in the right hand — left-handed use is generally considered abnormal. It is strictly forbidden to strike bowls or dishes with chopsticks, because this behaviour equates to begging for food. Never lay a bundle of chopsticks on the table in disorder, because it means death and bad luck; also do not put chopsticks upright into a bowl of rice, for this is part of the ritual of making sacrifice to deceased ancestors.

四合院 COURTYARD HOUSE

THE CHINESE QUADRANGLE or Chinese courtyard house (siheyuan) is a traditional Chinese compound. Built from grey bricks and tiles, it consists of one or more courtyards surrounded by four or more groups of chambers. While it is a representative structure in Beijing, it is also found in many other parts of the country, and the building structure is widely used in palaces, monasteries, and domestic and public buildings.

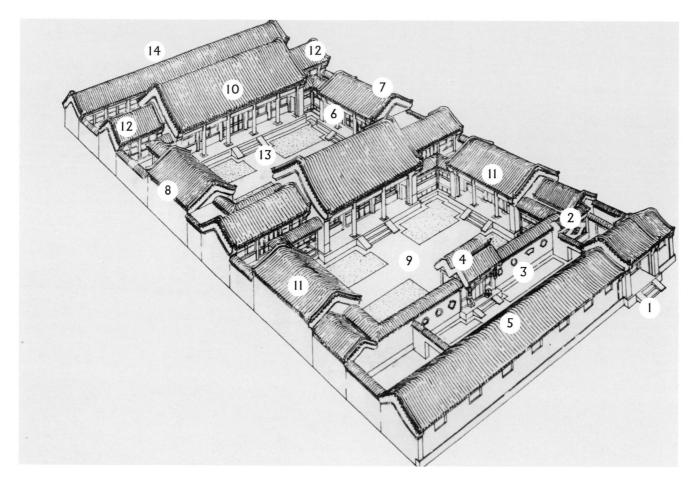

Among the variations of the Chinese quadrangle, the Beijing siheyuan is the most famous. The illustration shows its typical layout.

The Entrance Gate (1), or main entrance, is located on the southeastern corner of the compound. According to fengshui, this is a favorable position, blessed by the gentle and warm winds coming from the east and south.

The Screen Wall (2) inside the Entrance Gate is designed in consideration of privacy, and is often decorated with pot plants and a large goldfish bowl. Upon entering the gate and walking past the screen wall, one feels at once the tranquility and beauty of the compound.

There are four parts of courtyard in the compound: the Front Courtyard (3), the Central Courtyard (9), the Side Courtyards (11) and the Back Courtyard (13). The Central Courtyard, flanked by the two Side Courtyards, provides the largest open space in the compound. It is often decorated with various plants and fruit trees.

The Festoon Gate (4) is named for the front overhang of its roof, with two short suspended wooden shafts on each side and richly decorated with floral patterns. This gate separates the Front Courtyard (3) (the outer part of the compound) from the Central Courtyard (9) (the inner part of the compound). In terms of importance, the Festoon

Gate is second only to the Entrance Gate (1); therefore it is also called the "Second Gate".

The Roofed Pathways (6) link different chambers of a siheyuan together. On rainy days, they double as covered walkways, along which residents may take pleasant strolls. For insiders, the presence of Roofed Pathways is a key criterion for judging the authenticity of a siheyuan.

The Principal Chambers (10), which are located on the northern side of the compound, are the most sunlit and are typically inhabited by the elder of the family or the head of the household. There are usually three or more Principal Chambers. The central chamber, known as the "Central Hall" or "Bright Chamber", is most spacious and is used as the family's sitting room. The chambers on the two sides of the Central Hall serve as the bedrooms and study of the head of the household. The Principal Chambers are flanked by two wings which are known as the "Ear Chambers" (12), as their small size and low roof give them a semblance of a pair of ears (on the Principal Chambers).

On the eastern and western sides of the compound stand two rows of side chambers. The West Side Chambers (8) comprise the residential quarters of the eldest son and his wife. They are slightly higher than the East Side Chambers (7), where the younger sons and their spouses live. The row of chambers to the south side of the compound have a northern exposure to sunlight, facing the Principal Chambers (10); they are thus known as the "Opposite Chambers" (5). The chamber at the eastern end of the Entrance Gate is the residence of the private teacher (if the family is wealthy enough to hire one), while the chamber at the western end is used to receive arriving guests. The remaining Opposite Chambers are used to accommodate guests and male servants.

Located at the rear of the compound are a row of chambers known as the "Backside Chambers" (14), which have the same number of rooms as the "Opposite Chambers" (5). These are the residential quarters of the family's unmarried daughters and female servants.

Among other things, the composition of the siheyuan mirrors both the private nature of the Chinese family and the patriarchal structure of traditional Chinese society. As such, perhaps it is not difficult to see why emperors in the Forbidden City and their humble subjects in different parts of old Beijing lived in dwellings with basically the same configuration.

饺子 DUMPLINGS

THE CHINESE DUMPLING, or jiaozi, is a popular traditional food, consisting of mixed fillings wrapped in a thin piece of dough and sealed at the edges.

The dumpling has a very long history — dating as far back as two millennia. According to lore, it was invented by the great Chinese medicine man Zhang Zhongjing of the Eastern Han Dynasty (25–220). It is said that during one plague-ravaged winter, seeing the suffering in the countryside, Zhang concocted a special dumpling stuffed with mutton and herbs which he distributed to the poor. This concoction is the prototype of the modern-day dumpling.

Today, the dumpling is a part of the Spring Festival celebration, associated with reunion, hope and joy, and prepared on the eve of the lunar new year. Dumplings are arranged in circles when served, symbolizing togetherness. They can have a variety of fillings, ranging from pork and chicken to mutton and shrimp, often mixed with eggs and chopped vegetables, such as cabbage, celery, and leek.

Dumplings can be cooked in a variety of ways — boiled, steamed, or fried (the last of which are known as "potstickers" in North America). They are dipped into a sauce that always includes vinegar, and sometimes garlic, ginger and sesame oil. The dumpling should not be confused with the wonton: it has a thicker skin, and is bigger with denser fillings; the wonton, in contrast, is smaller and thinner, and known for its soft skin.

The dumpling is popular not only in China, but widely consumed in Southeast Asian countries as well, where there are delectable local variations.

火锅 HOT POT

HOT POT, OR HUOGUO, is a dish that enjoys vast popularity in China. The simple setup involves a "hot pot" of boiling water, into which rounds of raw meat and vegetables are thrown, then lifted out seconds later to be eaten with sauce. At the end of the session, which can last for hours, the pot of hot water becomes a delicious broth. On a freezing winter night, there is nothing cozier than gathering around a steaming hot pot with family and friends.

The hot pot has a long history and many regional varieties. The earliest hot pot as we know it dates back to almost two thousand years ago, unearthed in northern China, where hot pots were used to cook various kinds of meat and keep food warm in extremely cold weather. The hot pot became popular during the Song Dynasty, around 1000 AD. During the Qing Dynasty (1616—1911), it was introduced to the imperial court and became one of the emperors' favourite dishes. It is said that Emperor Qianlong was so fond of hot pot meals that wherever he went, his cooks would bring a pot with them. Once he even threw a banquet in the Forbidden Palace which served over five hundred people and utilized some one thousand and five hundred hot pots.

Among the regional variations of hot pot, the outstanding ones include the spicy hot pot of Sichuan, the seafood hot pot of Guangdong Province, the mutton hot pot of Beijing, and the chrysanthemum hot pot of Jiangsu and Zhejiang provinces. In Taiwan Province, people sometimes add seven ingredients to the hot pot, symbolizing seven qualities. The ingredients are celery, garlic, green onion, coriander, leek, fish and meat; the qualities are, respectively, diligence, wisdom, cleverness, popularity, everlasting happiness, abundance and affluence.

There are a number of traditions associated with serving hot pot. For example, in parts of northern China, food is placed in the pot with great care. If the family has an important guest, meat from fowl is put in the front of the pot, and other meats are placed in the back. Fish is placed on the left and shrimps on the right.

In the past, hot pots were heated with coal and wood. Today's electric hotpots, easily found in any supermarket, are safe, fast and clean. Supermarkets and food stores sell ready-made hot pot ingredients, such as ground pork, beef, chicken and fish balls. The dipping sauce can also be purchased pre-made.

The hot pot is popular not only in China but throughout Asia. Japan, Korea and Indonesia all have their own versions of hot pot.

麻将 MAHJONG

MEN OR WOMEN, old or young, Chinese people from all walks of life — ranging from farmers to teachers, factory workers to bankers, and even lawyers — like to gather and play mahjong in their spare time. As a carefree social pastime, mahjong is also sometimes associated with gambling. But no matter what people may think, mahjong occupies a remarkable place in Chinese culture.

The origin of mahjong is shrouded in myths. According to one conjecture, mahjong was invented by Confucius about 2,500 years ago. Supporters of this theory have drawn associations between the engraved designs on the tiles and elements of Confucian thought. Unfortunately, no real evidence supports this claim. Today, historians generally believe that mahjong in its modern form emerged during the 1850s, and probably evolved from a card game popular in the early 17th century.

west) and loong tiles (zhong, fa and bai). The flower tiles feature four plants (plum, orchid, bamboo and chrysanthemum) and the four seasons.

Mahjong is deeply rooted in Chinese daily life. During big gatherings of relatives and friends, mahjong is a favorite choice, as it easily gets many people involved, whether as players or as onlookers. Mahjong can be played almost everywhere, at home, in teahouses, and even around the street corner.

In 2002, the first World Mahjong Championship was held in Tokyo. The following year saw the first annual China Majiang Championship. The first Open European Mahjong Championships was held in the Netherlands in 2005.

Mahjong was introduced to the West in the early 1900s and turned out to be quite a fashion. Though the craze has

Mahjong features rectangular tiles with engravings on one side. The game is played with four players. At the beginning of the game, the tiles are shuffled face down, and each player stacks a row of tiles in front of him or her. The dealer throws two or three dice to decide where to start dealing the tiles. Each player is dealt thirteen tiles (the dealer has one extra), and then draws a tile and discards one in turn. The object of the game is to collect a winning combination before the others.

Playing mahjong involves calculation, strategy and luck. A set of tiles consists of 144 pieces in three categories, namely 108 suit tiles, 28 honour tiles and eight flower tiles. There are three suits: circles, stripes and wan, each numbered from one to nine. The suits are related to money: circles represent coins, stripes strings of coins, and wan, according to its literal meaning, "ten thousand coins". The honour tiles include wind tiles (labelled according to the four directions — north, south, east and

long faded out, mahjong reached many Western households for a time.

For those who want to find more about mahjong, *The Complete Book of Mah-jongg* by Alan D. Millington is a good source of information.

茅台 MAOTAI

THE ORIGIN OF CHINESE RICE WINE can be traced back over 5,000 years, and one name closely connected to its history is Maotai. Maotai wine is named after the town of the same name in Guizhou Province. First made as early as 2,000 years ago in the Han Dynasty, Maotai is regarded as the premier Chinese rice wine.

Its supreme quality won it a gold medal in the 1915 Panama Pacific International Exposition in San Francisco. Since then, Maotai has gained international recognition, and is regarded as one of the three best-known liquors in the world along with Scotch whisky and cognac. It is now regarded as the Chinese national wine and has been used on official occasions in receptions for foreign heads of state and distinguished guests. It is the only alcoholic beverage presented as an official gift by Chinese embassies in foreign countries and regions. It received additional exposure in China and abroad when Premier Zhou Enlai used the wine to entertain President Richard Nixon at the state banquet during his visit to China in 1972. Maotai now has gained in popularity among ordinary people all over the world. It has become one of the top-sellers in Chinese wine markets. More than 6,800 tons of Maotai were sold in 2007, and Guizhou Maotai Company sells over 200 tons of Maotai to over 100 countries each year.

Wine is one reflection of a country's history and culture. Chinese people love wine, no matter whether they are with friends or alone. Li Bai, the most famous poet in ancient China, wrote many poems under the inspiration of wine. One of Li Bai's most famous poems is *Drinking Alone by Moonlight*, which expresses the poet's feelings after becoming a little drunk. These are the first four verses of the poem:

> *A cup of wine, under the flowering trees;*
> *I drink alone, for no friend is near.*
> *Raising my cup I beckon the bright moon,*
> *She and I, with my shadow, will make three people.*

As one of the important names in Chinese wine history, many legends are linked to Maotai. Among them, the story of Maotai's origin is beautiful. On one Chinese New Year's Eve, it was windy and freezing and snowed heavily in Maotai Town. A young man called Li noticed an old woman in ragged clothes dying in front of his door. Kindly, Li helped the old woman home, prepared a delicious meal with rice wine for her, and gave his own bed to the woman. That night, Li had a dream in which he was awakened by pleasant music, and saw a goddess coming from the sky with a shining wine cup in her hands. When the goddess placed the wine in front of him, he smelled an odour delicate and pleasing, better than any he had ever savoured. The next morning, to his great surprise, the old woman had disappeared, and when he opened the door, a river lay in front of him. The water from the river gave off an odour like that in his dream. After that, people began to produce wine from the river's water.

Another popular legend arose in the 1970s during U.S. President Nixon's visit to China. Premier Zhou Enlai in the course of his dinner with President Nixon, showed Nixon how wine could be set aflame. Nixon was fascinated, and took two bottles of Maotai home. Back in the White House, Nixon tried to surprise his wife and daughter with the same trick. Unfortunately, the bowl

The town of Maotai in Guizhou Province

Right: The classic bottle of Maotai

that contained the spirits heated up and cracked, setting the tablecloth on fire. The heat set off the fire alarms in the building, and the incident gave root to the story that is still remembered today. Even Secretary of State Henry Kissinger admitted that the story is true.

Whether these legends are true or not, however, one thing that is most amazing is that women who live in the town of Maotai have exceptionally beautiful skin, and men who drink Maotai retain their youthful allure. Although alcohol is not good for people's health, the ingredients in Maotai seem to create a rare chemical reaction. American and Chinese scientists are currently trying to unravel the mystery.

旗袍 QIPAO

Modern qipao is a popular dress for Hollywood stars

QIPAO, the dress that has become an icon of traditional Chinese femininity, is in fact derived from the Manchu gown. During the 1920s and 1930s, the qipao became a popular fashion among the liberal-minded women of big cities. In its modern incarnation, the qipao is characterized by a high collar, front-right diagonal slit, tight-fitting waist and short sleeves, embodying at once sensuality and restraint.

The traditional Manchu gown that preceeded the modern qipao was a loose-fitting garment extending the length of the body, collarless with long sleeves. The one-piece gown, worn by both men and women, had a distinctly pastoral appearance, reflecting the nomadic origins of the Manchu people. With the establishment of the Qing Dynasty (1616–1911) by the Manchus, the Manchu costume was briefly imposed on all, but for the most part Han Chinese women continued to wear the two-piece traditional Han dress; the qipao thus drew an ethnic demarcation, as its name indicates — "the gown of the Qi (Manchus)". During the late Qing Dynasty, more elaborate forms of the qipao began to emerge, with the appearance of flourishes on the sleeves and the high collar known today.

The latter half of the 19th century was a momentous time for China, with Western invasion and the gradual collapse of the Qing Empire, culminating in the Republican Revolution of 1911, affecting almost all aspects of life. Fashion was no exception. The qipao, after fading into obscurity for some time, re-emerged in the 1920s as a bold fashion statement, incorporating elements from the traditional Han Chinese female two-piece dress. The popular qipao at this time had wide sleeves, revealing the wrist, and abandoned the ornate flourishes of the late Qing Dynasty for minimal patterns.

The qipao changed again in the late 1920s, popularized by both female students and new-era socialites of Shanghai. By this time it had become a symbol of female liberation, absorbing elements of Western attire. It became more tight-fitting, with a higher cut, and variations with short sleeves began to appear. In 1929, the qipao was declared an official Chinese dress, the female counterpart to the Sun Yat-sen suit for men.

The modern qipao known today is a versatile garment, serving as both inspiration for the catwalk and uniform among restaurant hostesses. It continues to be a dress of the times, re-interpreting and adapting tradition to modern uses and aesthetics.

Right: Traditional qipao

豆腐 TOFU

TOFU, OR BEAN CURD, IS A delectable, soy-based food that originated in China and spread to almost every corner of the world. This ostensibly simple food is very rich in taste, nutrition and cultural background.

Legend has it that around 200 BC, a Chinese emperor wanted to have eternal life, so he had many people making magical herbal concoctions for him. When they experimented with soy, they invented tofu by sheer chance. It turned out that they discovered one of the most tasty foods in history (in spite of their failure to find the elixir of immortality). The place where they invented tofu, in present-day Anhui Province, has since become known as the hometown of tofu, and remains one of the best places to taste tofu today. During the Qing Dynasty (1616–1911), when Emperor Kangxi came to inspect the neighbouring areas he prepared a secret gift for his ministers. The gift was neither gold nor silver, which he had often given them, but delicious local tofu.

When tofu travelled across China to different regions, people adopted many different ways of cooking it. Famous variants include the spicy tofu of Sichuan, the mirror tofu of Wuxi, and Yangzhou's shredded tofu with chicken soup. Perhaps the most distinct variant is Nanjing's stinky tofu. As its name suggests, the stinky tofu absolutely stinks, but it is not because it has gone bad, but because of the spices added to the mix. People are usually horrified by the smell, but when they start eating the stinky tofu, they simply cannot stop. In Nanjing, it is not uncommon to see folks devouring the stinky tofu while standing beside the vendor.

The influence of tofu has gone far beyond food culture. In Chinese, there are many sayings associated with this food. "As soft as tofu" is used to describe a soft-hearted or feeble-minded person. When young people joke that they wish to commit suicide, they will say something like "let me find a piece of tofu and knock myself against it".

Since the Tang Dynasty (618–907), tofu has been exported to many parts of the world. Today, soy-based foods such as tofu have become staples of vegetarian and vegan diets. The protein content of tofu is almost as high as that of fish and beef, but soy protein is easier to absorb. Compared to meat, tofu contains little cholesterol, and has various amino acids needed by the human body. The versatility of tofu is evident in modern forms like tofu salad, tofu burger, tofu cookies and even tofu ice cream.

蒙古包 YURT

THE YURT IS THE TRADITIONAL dwelling of Mongolians and also found in other parts of Central Asia. It is a tent-like structure consisting of a circular wooden frame covered by a thick piece of felt fastened from the outside with ropes. Sometimes the felt strip is white and decorated with red, blue, yellow or another coloured cloth. The roof of the yurt is a domed crown. The entire structure is kept under compression by the weight of the covers, sometimes supplemented by a heavy weight suspended from the centre of the roof. Yurts vary in size, with their capacity ranging from a dozen to hundreds of people.

The functionality and versatility of the yurt is related to the nomadic lifestyle. It is easy to assemble and take apart, and transported by animals such as horses, camels and yaks. The domed crown makes it difficult for rain and snow to accumulate on top of the yurt in spite of inclement weather.

The wooden crown of the yurt is emblematic. In old Kazakh communities, while the yurt itself is repaired and rebuilt frequently, the crown remains intact, passed down from generation to generation. Its history is observable through the accumulation of smoke stains on the crown.

Today, the yurt has become a symbol of Mongolians, as well as of many other ethnic groups in China.

A row of Mongolian yurts

6

ARTS & CRAFTS

文学艺术

清明上河图 ALONG THE RIVER DURING THE QINGMING FESTIVAL

ALONG THE RIVER during the Qingming Festival is the name of a panoramic painting by Zhang Zeduan (1085–1145), an artist of the Song Dynasty (960–1279). Known as "China's Mona Lisa", it is probably the single most widely known artwork in China. The piece, painted in hand-scroll format with ink on silk, vividly depicts daily life along the Bian River in the Northern Song Dynasty capital, Bianjing (present-day Kaifeng, in Henan Province). With its encyclopedic range of subjects, from people and animals to period architecture and folk customs, it provides a glimpse into the life of the period.

The original painting measures 9.8in (24.8cm) in width and over 16ft (5m) in length, depicting 814 individual figures, 60 animals, 28 boats, 20 vehicles, nine sedan chairs, 30 buildings and 170 trees. The urban and the rural areas constitute the two main sections of the picture, with the Bian River meandering through the entire length. In the left half of the painting, which depicts the town, are bustling shops and boisterous crowds. At the centre of the painting stands a grand bridge, busy with commerce. All kinds of folks can be spotted here — officials, servants, peddlers, bakers, shopkeepers and even beggars. The main

vehicles for transportation are also vividly depicted, including sedan chairs, wheelbarrows, and carts drawn by bulls, horses or donkeys. In the right half of the painting lie the rural outskirts, with their peaceful fields, cottages and unhurried farmers.

The painting is valued for its detailed, geometrically accurate depictions of buildings and objects, beautifully juxtaposed against the flowing lines of the mountains, water and fields. The theme of the painting celebrates the worldly commotion during the Qingming Festival, a traditional Chinese holiday in April when people mourn the deceased and celebrate connections to their ancestors.

Over the centuries, the painting has been the subject of various palace intrigues, thefts and wars. Forgers could pass off their copies, partly because the original version was repeatedly stolen from the imperial collection. Pu Yi, the last emperor of the Qing Dynasty, was especially fond of the painting, and took it with him when he was forced to leave the Forbidden City in 1924. In the following years of social turbulence, the painting went missing until it was found by chance in 1950. It is now kept at the Palace Museum in Beijing.

Part of the scroll, Along the River during the Qingming Festival, by Zhang Zeduan (1085—1145)

青花瓷 BLUE-AND-WHITE PORCELAIN

CHINA HAS LONG BEEN celebrated for its exquisite porcelain, which is why porcelain is also called china in English. Blue-and-white porcelain refers to white porcelain decorated with blue pigment — most often cobalt oxide. It is made as follows: the porcelain piece is dried and then decorated with refined cobalt-blue pigment mixed with water, coated with a clear glaze, and finally fired at a temperature of around 1,300°C.

The first blue-and-white porcelain wares were made as early as in the Tang Dynasty (618–907). The manufacturing techniques matured in the Yuan Dynasty (1206–1368) when fine and translucent blue-and-white porcelain was mass produced at the town of Jingde, which is traditionally known as the Capital of Porcelain. Blue-and-white porcelain continued to prosper in the Ming Dynasty (1368–1644) and, as is generally agreed, reached the height of its technical excellence during the reign of Emperor Kangxi (1654–1722) in the Qing Dynasty.

In the Yuan Dynasty, blue-and-white porcelain was exported in large quantities to West Asia, where its beauty won the hearts of the upper class; in fact, many patterns were designed to cater to foreign tastes. By the beginning of the 17th century, blue-and-white porcelain had aroused great enthusiasm in European courts and was avidly collected by kings and princes. Today, many of the best Yuan Dynasty blue-and-white porcelain examples are kept in museums in Turkey and Iran.

Blue-glazed vase with white dragon and flower pattern

青铜器 BRONZES

CHINESE BRONZES, or qing tong qi, symbolize the extraordinary art and technology of ancient China. When bronze was used mainly for agriculture and warfare in the rest of the world, the ancient Chinese made bronze into a variety of vessels and utensils for daily use and ritual services.

In most ancient civilizations including China, bronze was widely used because of its relatively low melting point as well as its strength and durability. Archaeological findings suggest that Chinese people started making bronze utensils from the Xia Dynasty (ca. 2070–1600 BC). The bronzes produced between the 15th century BC and the 10th century BC were claimed to be the most artistic. They were moulded into all kinds of shapes, and were delicately decorated with lengthy and complicated inscriptions. Some bronzes were inscribed with an essay of more than four hundred Chinese characters. After the Zhou Dynasty (1029 BC–256 BC), bronzes were gradually replaced by iron and china.

The production of bronzes in ancient China reached an unparalleled artistic and technological level. For instance, the inscriptions on the bronzes included images of various kinds of animals. For some, the entire bronze was moulded as an animal or a monster in mythology. Names of important people were also inscribed onto the bronzes. One famous bronze shaped as an owl had the name Fuhao on it. Fuhao was a heroine and the wife of an emperor. Legend had it that she led armies sweeping across a number of kingdoms. The bronze was buried in the tomb after her death.

Chinese bronzes could be divided into a number of categories according to their uses, such as sacrificial vessels, wine vessels, food vessels, water vessels, musical instruments, weapons and currencies. Each kind could be further divided. For wine vessels, there were over ten types, depending on the shape and capacity. The ancient Chinese also learned how to fuse bronze and iron to make stronger and more durable tools. A sword uncovered in Henan Province was made of a mixture of bronze and iron with a fairly accurate proportion. It was believed to have been produced as early as around 800 BC.

Chinese bronzes brought artistic work into average family homes. More than ten thousand inscribed bronzes have been uncovered, not to mention those without inscriptions. They represent a perfect marriage between art and daily life. When the ancient people were enjoying food and drinks, they could at the same time appreciate the artistic beauty of the utensils. It must have been a truly enjoyable experience.

Bronze galloping horse

Sanxingdui head portrait

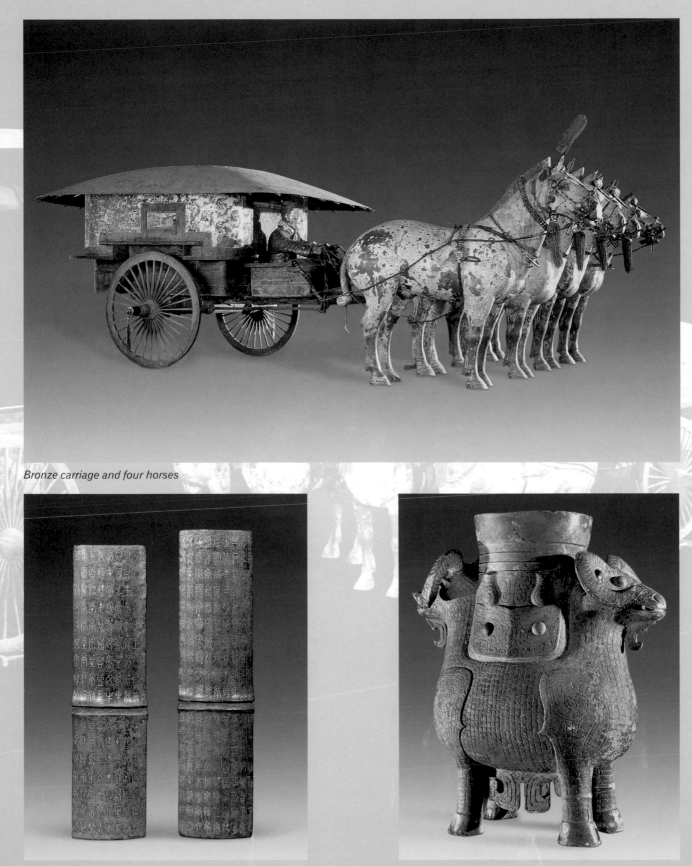

Bronze carriage and four horses

Bronze Ejunqi Tally

Two-sheep zun (drinking cup)

编钟 CHIME BELLS

CHIME BELLS ARE a form of ancient percussion instrument, hanging on the bell frame in groups in order of size and sound. Dating back to as early as the Shang Dynasty over 3,500 years ago, they prevailed as the major musical instrument during the period of Warring States (475–221 BC). Only the nobility could enjoy the privilege of owning chime bells, which thus became a symbol of status and power.

Originally a set of chime bells only had three pieces, but gradually the number increased so as to produce more complex music.

Up until now, the largest set of chime bells discovered are the ones unearthed in the tomb of Marquis Yi of the Zeng State, made about 2,500 years ago. Altogether the set comprises 65 bronze bells, divided into eight groups. The huge bell frame is about 36ft (11m) long and 9ft (2.7m) tall with the bells arranged on it in three layers, the smallest on the top and the biggest at the base. The largest bell is 5ft (152.3cm) tall and weighs 450 pounds (203.6kg); the smallest one is only 8 in (20.2cm) and weighs 5.3 pounds (2.4kg). All the bells are decorated with colourful patterns.

This set of bells still works quite well today, with amazingly accurate pitch and excellent timbre. The set covers a range of five octaves from C2 to D7, is capable of tone modulation, and each bell can produce two distinct tones when struck differently. A team of five is needed to strike these bells with wooden mallets. The inscription on the bells tells where to place each bell, how to play them, and the tones of each bell. There are altogether 28 tone names and 66 syllable names, providing good material for the study of ancient Chinese music.

红楼梦 DREAM OF THE RED CHAMBER

DREAM OF THE RED CHAMBER is a masterpiece of classical Chinese literature, a semi-autobiographical novel attributed to the Qing Dynasty writer Cao Xueqin, who lived during the 18th century. The novel depicts the fall of the Jia family from its glorious days of imperial patronage, reflecting the decline of Cao's own family and age. It portrays in sophisticated detail the complex interpersonal relationships and interwoven psychologies among the members of a large Chinese family.

The central protagonist of the novel is Jia Baoyu, named after the jade that issued from his mouth at birth. Indulged by his family, Baoyu grew to resent worldly pursuits such as fame and power, and instead spent his time with his female cousins and maids, whom he saw as the embodiment of beauty and purity. He once said that his greatest regret was having been born a man. A substantial part of the novel is devoted to describing Baoyu's romance with Lin Daiyu, a doomed love opposed by the family elders in an age of arranged marriage. Daiyu was beautiful and frail, affecting a proud and solitary disposition. Her fragile physique is compared to the slim boughs of a willow swaying in the wind, and her emotions are equally delicate. In one memorable scene, she mourns and buries the petals of fallen flowers, thinking perhaps of the evanescence of her own youth and beauty. Eventually, her frailty would not survive the tumultuous turns of the familial destiny.

Among the many memorable characters of the novel, two others stand out — the intelligent and tactful Xue Baochai, Daiyu's friend and also rival for Baoyu's love, who married Baoyu; and Wang Xifeng, the matriarch of the family, who appears at times shrewd and vicious.

During the last century, the novel has been made into more than twenty films, soap operas and TV series. Numerous books have been published on the subject, and an entire branch of Chinese literary scholarship is devoted to the study of the novel.

刺绣 EMBROIDERY

CIXIU, or Chinese embroidery, is a traditional ornamental art. Changsha, the capital of Hunan Province, is known for its history of Chinese silk stitching. Here, embroidered fabrics of the State of Chu (Warring States Period, 475–221 BC), unearthed in 1958, are believed to be the earliest records of Chinese embroidery.

The four major schools of embroidery in China are associated with various localities — Jiangsu, Hunan, Guangdong and Sichuan. For centuries Chinese embroidery has been appreciated in the West, and has appeared at various international fairs. The first prize-winner of Chinese embroidery in an international competition was from Guangdong, honoured at the London World Exposition in 1851.

At the South China Commodity Fair of 1910 in Nanjing, attended by some 200,000 visitors, a woman named Shen Shou became widely known. An iconic figure of Chinese embroidery representative of the Suzhou school, Shen (1874–1921) was recognized by the imperial court as a master craftswoman and later achieved prominence at various expositions around the world. She is remembered by the Western world for her portrait of Queen Elena of Italy (Helen of Montenegro, wife to Vittorio Emanuelle III), and a portrait of Jesus Christ at his crucification. She devoted her later life to teaching the art of embroidery in Nantong, Jiangsu Province.

While in ancient times wearing embroidery was an emblem of status and privilege, consumers of the 21st century benefit from the ready availability of beautiful embroidery. Modern Chinese embroidery is undergoing a technological revolution. Digitalized manufacturing has facilitated its mass production, while skilled craftsmanship and hand stitching techniques are treasured to this day.

中国结 KNOTTING (CHINESE KNOTS)

AS EARLY AS the Warring States Period (475–221 BC), patterns of Chinese knotting began to appear on bronze vessels, stone carvings and silk paintings. These are the first evidence of this folk art, though some archaeologists believe the art of tying knots can be dated back to prehistoric times. In ancient times, the knots were usually intended for keeping warm or recording events. The art later gained popularity since the Ming Dynasty (1368–1644) and was used more often for ornament.

The Chinese knot is a distinctive and traditional Chinese folk handicraft. In Chinese, "knot" (Pinyin: "jie") indicates reunion, friendliness, peace, warmth, marriage and love. Therefore, a Chinese knot is a way to express good wishes such as happiness, prosperity and love. The knots can come in a variety of colours — gold, green, blue and yellow; however, the most common choice is red, which also symbolizes good luck and prosperity in Chinese culture.

One major characteristic of this artwork is that any knot is made out of only one thread. When finished, the knot looks identical from both the right and left, from the front and back. According to legend, a monk, who is said to be the inventor of modern Chinese knots, used one thread together with jade and other decorations to make a knot to represent his whole-hearted devotion to Buddhism. Viewed from any perspective, his admiration for Buddha was the same.

There are many different shapes of Chinese knots, which are based on several basic knotting techniques. The most popular shapes include butterflies, flowers, fish and shoes. These shapes are thought to have magic powers, and each of them matches with a particular good wish. Many Chinese artworks express good wishes making use of puns, and Chinese knots follow this practice. The character "fish" correlates to "prosperity" in Chinese, and therefore a fish knot represents wealth; "bat" is pronounced the same as "good luck", and a bat knot conveys that meaning. Some other knots are expected to work as a bagua mirror, which will ward off evil spirits. Such knots include the Pan Chang Knot and the Good Luck Knot.

Since ancient times, the Chinese knot has been used for various occasions — from palace halls to countryside households, from everyday decoration to special celebrations like the wedding ceremony. Besides hanging on the walls, Chinese knots are also used to decorate corners of chairs or other furniture, edges of parasols, streamers attached to the waistbands of lady's dresses, and all manners of seals, mirrors, pouches, sachets, eyeglass cases, fans, and Buddhist rosaries. In *Dream of the Red Chamber*, one of the four great classical novels of China, the author vividly describes the procedure of tying Chinese knots and their functions.

The Chinese knots, with their classical elegance, reflect the grace and depth of Chinese culture. It makes this Chinese folk art one of the best gifts for friends both at home and abroad.

Chinese knots

甲骨文 ORACLE BONE INSCRIPTIONS

ORACLE BONES ARE pieces of bone or turtle shells that were heated and cracked, using a bronze pin, and then inscribed with what is known as oracle bone script. The oracle bone inscriptions, known as the earliest Chinese writing, are the ancient Chinese characters carved on turtle shells or animal scapulas. In the late Shang Dynasty (1600–1046 BC), the inscriptions were used mainly for divination and keeping records of events.

The oracle bone inscriptions were first found in 1899 by the scholar Wang Yirong. Some unknown characters on the "loong bones", one of the ingredients of his medicine, caught his attention. The bones were then traced to Anyang in Henan Province, the capital of the late Shang Dynasty, where over 150,000 oracle bone inscriptions have been excavated.

A great deal of knowledge of the Shang Dynasty has been learned from the study of these oracle bone inscriptions, and many books about them have been published. A good collection of the inscriptions can be found in the *Encyclopedia of Oracle Bone Inscriptions*, compiled by a team headed by Guo Moruo. It includes 41,956 inscriptions selected from the oracle bone inscriptions discovered before 1973. The 13 volumes of the book were published in 1978 and 1982. Thanks to the efforts of many scholars, about 2,000 characters among the more than 4,500 found on the bones have been identified. The remaining unidentified characters are mainly place names and people's names.

The inscriptions were used mainly for divination during the Shang Dynasty. The rulers of the Shang Dynasty were very superstitious so divination was basically a daily activity for almost everything, including weather, health, farming and fortune. The bones were used in divination not only as a tool, but also for recording the results. The inscriptions were usually classified into four categories — classes and country, society and production, culture, and others.

Left: Characters inscribed in about 1600–1000 BC
Below: Oracle bone inscriptions on display

剪纸 PAPER CUTTING

ONE OF CHINA'S most popular folk arts is paper-cutting, with its origin closely connected to the invention of paper during the Han Dynasty (206 BC–221 AD). The paper-cut is a picture cut out of a piece of paper using scissors. The picture patterns are often pasted over lintels, windows, or lanterns to express the feelings of joy and observations of life.

Paper-cut is also called "window flower" or "cutting picture" and can cover a wide range of themes from historical legend to ancient myth. It is exquisite in conception, simple and unadorned in shape and vigorous in line, and speaks strongly of traditional Chinese values. Styles vary from region to region; the paper-cut in South China is delicate and beautiful, while in North China it is robust and energetic.

As paper was highly precious in the early days it could be afforded only by the wealthy, so the art of paper cutting first became popular in the royal palaces and houses of the nobility as a favourite pastime for court ladies. Later, as paper became cheaper (between the 7th and 13th centuries), paper cutting was immensely popular during folk festivals and celebrations. In the 14th century the art spread to the Middle East and Europe; and from the 15th century onward, paper cutting had become an integral part of everyday life for many people. But during the 19th century paper cutting almost disappeared altogether as old China experienced successive years of disastrous wars brought on by domestic turmoil and foreign invasion.

The Chinese make paper-cuts for celebrations, festivals and home decoration, with the extensive use of red, which is the lucky colour in China. Popular themes include the animals of the Chinese zodiac or a single or just a couple of Chinese characters. Paper-cuts can also be used in religious ceremonies.

Paper-cuts are primarily used as decoration: they ornament walls, windows, doors, columns, mirrors, lamps and lanterns in homes across China and are also used to embellish presents or are given as presents. Because the paper-cut is mostly pasted on the window, people generally name it "the paper-cut window decoration". For Spring Festival (the traditional Chinese New Year), many ordinary people like sticking different kinds of paper-cuts on their windows and by doing so, paper-cut window decoration not only celebrates the jubilant festive atmosphere, but also brings aesthetic enjoyment to people.

紫砂壶 PURPLE CLAY TEAPOT

AMONG THE MOST famous ceramics in China, purple clay teapots are made from a unique purple clay in the region of Yixing, a city in Jiangsu Province. This fine clay can be found only in this region and contains much iron. It is one of the best clays for making high-quality teapots, and is mostly reddish brown, light yellow or blackish purple.

Purple clay teapots can improve the flavour of tea. The more the teapots are used, the better quality they have. Purple clay teapots can be exchanged as precious gifts and serve as collectibles.

Purple clay teapots have been in use since the Song Dynasty (960–1279). They gradually became popular in the Ming Dynasty (1368–1644) and Qing Dynasty (1616–1911). Simple and harmonious geometric designs can always be found on teapots from the Ming Dynasty. Ceramic techniques were not developed as today; the teapots were rarely without blemishes, but the elegance of the vessel was highlighted by the rough particles on the surface. The colours were always reddish brown or purple grey. Gong Chun, Li Zhongfang, Shi Dabin and Xu Youquan were four of the masters of purple clay teapot making. They have made a great contribution to the development of teapot-making techniques.

As people began to brew tea instead of boiling it, purple clay teapots became more popular in daily life. It was a good choice for tea brewing. The teapot can absorb the tea fragrance and retain it for a long time. The longer the teapot is used, the better the flavour. The purple clay teapot also has aesthetic value, and is popular among ceramics lovers and collectors all over the world.

A hexahedral purple teapot

三国演义 THE ROMANCE OF THE THREE KINGDOMS

Liu Bei went to visit Zhuge Liang three times to ask for the latter's assistance

THE ROMANCE OF THE THREE KINGDOMS is one of the Four Great Novels of ancient China, together with *The Journey to the West*, *The Water Margin* and *Dream of the Red Chamber*. In one hundred and twenty chapters, this historical novel vividly portrays the turbulent era of the Three Kingdoms (220–280), bringing to life more than a thousand characters against a mottled canvas of political intrigues, intricate rivalries and epic battles.

The main rivalry of the novel lies between Liu Bei, the king of Shu, and Cao Cao, the minister of Wei. Liu was cherished for his benevolence to his people and loyalty to his friends, which won him numerous followers and aided his rise to power. Before his army grew strong he was often threatened by enemy forces, yet the local villagers would always flee with him when he was forced to abandon a town. He was aided by five powerful warrior-generals, among them the proud and loyal Guan Yu and the hot-tempered Zhang Fei. On the other side, Cao Cao, Liu Bei's lifelong enemy, was extremely cunning and deceitful. He held the emperor of the Eastern Han Dynasty as his hostage, and attempted to rule the entire country on his behalf. In contrast to the evil usurper in the novel, the historical figure of Cao Cao was actually an outstanding strategist, statesman, military commander and poet.

The era of the Three Kingdoms was fraught with battles. The novel contains superb descriptions of war, ranging from large-scale battles involving hundreds of thousands of soldiers to spectacular one-on-one martial confrontations. Yet it is the distinct personalities and abilities of the heroes, and not the actual scenes of battle, that are most memorable. For instance, in the episode titled "Guan Yu Defeating Hua Xiong before the Liquor Cooled Down", few readers will recall the actual details of how Guan chopped off Hua's head, but all are impressed by Guan's deftness, for he managed to behead a prestigious enemy general in a lightning attack. In the episode "Capturing Meng Huo Seven Times", what is most impressive is not exactly how the strategist Zhuge Liang managed to defeat and capture Meng Huo seven times in a row, but how he was wise enough to foresee a potential ally in Meng, for after capturing and releasing him seven times, Meng gave up rebelling and became utterly faithful to the Kingdom of Shu.

The Romance of the Three Kingdoms has inspired many re-interpretations and spin-offs in Chinese popular culture. China Central Television spent almost five years shooting an epic TV series based on the novel, with eighty-four episodes and employing over four hundred thousand crew. Movies, pop songs and animated cartoons and video games continue to introduce the characters of the novel to the young, who often refer to the novel, instead of historical records (such as the *Chronology of the Three Kingdoms*), for historical stories.

An opera based on the Battle of Chibi, between northern warlord Cao Cao and the allied southern warlords Liu Bei and Sun Quan

宋词 SONG CI

A ci by Chairman Mao Zedong

SONG CI refers to a kind of poetic lyrics that rose to popularity during the Song Dynasty (960–1279). Intimately influenced by Tang poetry, Song ci is freer in form, with lines of irregular lengths adhering to defined melodic patterns, often serving as lyrics to song. The voluminous collection of ci produced during the Song Dynasty sees a wide range of subjects and compositional styles, with about a hundred common melodic patterns.

Ci was usually sung in melody at private banquets and gatherings. Because of its close association with entertaining, the early ci were often themed around courtship and romance. Liu Yong, one of the most famous ci composers, wrote many romantic lyrics. Later, with the rise of literary masters like Su Shi, the ci expanded to include broader subjects such as war and statesmanship. Hailing from a famed literary family, and having passed the highest-level imperial examinations at a very young age, Su Shi held a variety of government posts for twenty years, yet experienced much political dissatisfaction. The heroic spirit and transcendence in his lyrics conveyed a strong sense of disappointment with the rulers of the day and frustration with thwarted political ambitions.

Among the host of ci composers, Li Qingzhao emerges as a brilliant female composer and one of China's foremost poets of all time. Her work was widely recognized before she was married at the age of 26. The absence of her beloved husband, who was often away travelling during his career as a government official, inspired many touching lyrics. His death would mark a turn in her lyrical style, which shifted from depictions of romantic affection to overwhelming loneliness and sadness.

Some of the most memorable Song ci were written by generals — Xin Qiji, a military commander, was an outstanding lyricist, as was Yue Fei, a general who was esteemed as a great patriot in history. Known to almost every Chinese, Yue Fei composed a piece of ci in a pattern named the "River of Red", a stirring classic filled with patriotism and optimism.

石狮子 STONE LIONS

IN CHINA, one finds imposing stone lions at the gates of important buildings such as government offices, banks, temples and big companies. Typically, the male lion crouches on the left with his right paw upon a ball, while the lioness sits on the right side with her left paw caressing a cub. Sometimes the ball and cub are absent, and the lions' postures vary from sitting to standing. What are these stone lions for?

In China, the lion has traditionally been a symbol of wealth and power. Having been introduced from West Asia during the first century, it acquired a deified status in Chinese culture, embodying the regal and the divine, sometimes associated with the spread of Buddhism.

It is believed that stone lions placed at the gate keep evil beings away. Myth has it that the lions' eyes would turn red or bleed before natural disasters, warning people of the coming danger.

Traditionally, the right to install stone lions is reserved for the rich and powerful.

A well-known pair are the lions at Tian'anmen Gate, the main entrance of the Forbidden City. During dynastic times, the lumps of curly hair on the stone lions indicated the ranks of the officials whose gates they guarded. The higher the rank, the more lumps on the heads of the lions. During the Ming Dynasty (1368–1644), the highest-ranking officials possessed lions with thirteen lumps of hair. Stone lions were forbidden to lower-ranking officials, not to say ordinary people.

In traditional Chinese architecture, stone lions are a popular motif on bridges. The best known example is Lugouqiao Bridge in Beijing, first built nearly a thousand years ago. Visitors will find anywhere between 485 and 501 stone lions crouching on the 140 posts of the bridge (the exact number remains debated), each possessing a unique design.

唐诗 TANG POETRY

MORE THAN A MILLENNIUM after the *Book of Poetry*, the Tang Dynasty (618–907) marked the golden age of classical Chinese poetry. With its dramatic rise and fall, its rich and often cosmopolitan cultural climate, and its flourishing literary culture, the Tang Dynasty not only provided an ideal setting for the production of literature but exceedingly rich subject matter as well. Today, the teeming collection of poems from the period, known collectively as Tang poetry, are distinct for their sound and form, while adopting diverse subjects, from love and war to nature and everyday life.

The compilation *Complete Tang Poems* records in excess of forty eight thousand pieces, composed by more than two thousand three hundred poets. The poems are derived from earlier song forms, adopting strict rhyme schemes and tonal structures. They generally consist of four or eight lines, with five or seven characters (and syllables) in each line. While the schemes appear to be strictly ordered, the tonal and rhyme patterns actually provided lilt and lyricism, adapted dramatically by great poets such the quintessential Tang poet Li Bai (701–762).

The abundant literary production of the Tang is by no means accidental. The early Tang witnessed unprecedented prosperity, with expanded frontiers, cosmopolitan influences coming by way of the Silk Road, and exposure to diverse world religions. The composition of poetry was integral to the imperial examinations and promoted by a flourishing literary culture. Early Tang poetry is marked by the abandonment of earlier sentimentalism and attention to the robustness of language.

The second stage of Tang poetry arrived as the Tang reached the height of its economic and cultural development during the 8th century. Poems written during this period depicted subjects of everyday life, as well as border skirmishes, which would later escalate and contribute to dynastic decline. Seemingly mundane subjects like visiting a friend or going fishing conveyed subtle and complex messages, such as dissatisfaction with the power struggles in court.

The last century of the Tang, marked by decadence among the ruling class and frequent border strife, and finally the An Lu Shan Rebellion (755–763), appeared in late Tang poetry with its full turbulence and devastation. The great poet Du Fu (712–770), who lived during this time, wrote about the despair among the populace, frequently invoking the image of a poet aching for his people in their plight.

The influence of Tang poetry is wide and far-reaching, inspiring later literary forms such as the ci of the Song Dynasty. Today, Tang poetry remains an essential part of the Chinese language curriculum in schools across the country. The poems provide not only aesthetic inspiration but vivid witness to a unique time in Chinese history.

The Yellow Crane Tower in the city of Wuhan, of which the poet Li Bai wrote a poem entitled "Seeing off Meng Haoran for Guangling at Yellow Crane Tower"

唐三彩 TANG TRI-COLOUR POTTERY

TANG TRI-COLOUR pottery, the tri-coloured pottery of the Tang Dynasty (618–907), is a type of glazed pottery known for its vibrant glints of green, yellow and brown. Stylistically naturalistic, with harmonious lines, Tang tri-colour pottery reflects the diverse influences and prosperity brought by trade along the Silk Road. During the early Tang, tri-colour glazed objects were exported to Eurasia, the Middle East and to many other countries in Asia.

The distinct hues of Tang tri-colour pottery were produced by adding metallic oxides to the glaze. Objects were fired in low-temperature kilns (heated to about 800°C), where the glaze changed gradually during the process of calcination, producing various colours. The dominant hues of yellow, brown and green appeared variegated and harmonious. Because of its fragility, Tang tri-colour pottery was generally used for burial objects, while daily objects were made in the more durable blue-and-white porcelain.

Tang tri-colour pottery was produced in Xi'an, Luoyang and Yangzhou, some of the most prosperous cities along the Silk Road. The camel, the primary vehicle of trade on this ancient route, was a dominant motif. A famous Tang tri-colour artefact unearthed from a general's tomb depicts a long-haired brown camel with a troupe of entertainers seated on its back — four musicians and a dancer in the middle. Playing various instruments, the musicians appear to have deep eyes, high-bridged noses and full beards, wearing white boots and different coloured sweaters with turned-down collars. Their exotic appearance is suggestive of the Eurasian and Middle Eastern influences which came by way of the Silk Road during this period.

Tang tri-colour camel with musicians

唐卡 TANGKA

THE TANGKA is a Tibetan religious painting. It is often mounted on soft materials such as silk, cloth and canvas, so that it is easily rolled up for storage and transport. The tangka is displayed for diverse purposes — from meditation and teaching to decoration. The religious stories illustrated in splendid colours often infuse a room with spiritual solemnity.

There are two types of tangka. One type is woven or embroidered; the other type is drawn, employing long-lasting dyes extracted from minerals. The tangka is primarily a religious object of Tibetan Buddhism, depicting Buddhas and Bodhisattvas. The later tangkas have extended their subjects to historical stories and local customs, with the works usually being unsigned.

A Tibetan Buddhist uses the tangka for meditation, which inspires his or her religious experience. Lamas and other Tibetan Buddhist tutors also use the tangka to educate their students, as they did in the past when literacy was little promoted.

Today, the tangka is treated with a combination of religious veneration and artistic awe. Tourists have acquired a taste for tangka as souvenirs.

Left: Thousand-hand Bodhisattva Avalokiteshvara

Below: Padmasambhava

水浒 THE WATER MARGIN

THE WATER MARGIN, one of the Four Great Novels of classical Chinese literature, is attributed to Shi Nai'an, who lived during the turbulent period at the end of the Yuan Dynasty (1206–1368) and the early Ming Dynasty (1368–1644). The famed tale of one hundred and eight outlaws, set during the the Northern Song Dynasty (960–1127), mirrored the strife-ridden countryside of Shi's own time, when peasants rose up in many places to rebel against the corrupt ruling class. The book, with its themes of brotherhood and loyalty, struggle and betrayal, is remarkable for its sophisticated plot, subtle political commentary, and its many memorable characters.

The Water Margin can be divided roughly into three parts. The first section portrays the corrupt ruling class of the Northern Song Dynasty. Gao Qiu, for instance, was promoted to power simply because he was good at soccer and thus favoured by the emperor. The book then moves on to describe how the ruling class exploited and abused ordinary folk, a number of whom went on to become outlaws. They met on Liang Mountain and formed a revolutionary troop, headed by Song Jiang, who escaped execution for his anti-court writings. Interestingly, Song had previously worked in the government, as had several other leaders of the rebel army. Lin Chong was once the chief coach of the imperial guard in the capital, and Lu Junyi used to be the wealthiest person in town. Both had very high status in the social hierarchy before they were set up by their enemies and had no choice but to flee to Liang Mountain. The outlaws came from all levels of society. Despite their radically different backgrounds, the outlaws shared the same aspiration for justice, robbing from the privileged and giving to the poor.

The Water Margin was a controversial book, banned by several imperial courts in case their subjects put the story into practice. In the 1920s, Pearl S. Buck produced an English translation entitled *All Men Are Brothers*, drawing from the Confucian ethics of a common fraternity. The novel has been adapted into a number of TV series, movies, cartoons and video games, and remains popular throughout East Asia.

On his way home, Wu Song passes by Jingyang Ridge and kills the fierce tiger there with bare hands

Lu Zhishen, the "Flowery Monk", one of the lead characters in The Water Margin, uproots a willow

LEGEND

神话传说

财神 CAI SHEN

YOU MAY HAVE HEARD about "Kung Hei Fa Choy", the most popular blessing to the Chinese during Spring Festival, which means "I wish you a wealthy New Year". However, you may not know one of the most venerated Chinese gods related to the blessing, Cai Shen.

Cai Shen (also pronounced as "choy sun" in Cantonese and "Tsai Shen Yeh" in Mandarin) literally means the God of Wealth in the Chinese pantheon. Dedicated to bringing profit and prosperity and fending off illness, he is so popular that you can find his statuette in many Chinese and East Asian houses and buildings, especially in family-run businesses such as shops, restaurants or hair salons. The incarnation of the Chinese God of Wealth is somewhat complicated and theologists and folklorists believe that Cai Shen has been presiding over a cabinet of his "treasury department" for thousands of years. Several minor deities under his authority are responsible for different areas of the fortune issue. For this reason, people may choose different deities of wealth in their houses based on their beliefs and needs.

Cai Shen, alias Zhao Gongming, originated in Taoism. He is often juxtaposed with the Three Stars Gods. He has a tanned face, dresses as a Taoist priest and often appears sitting on a tiger with a sword in his hand. He is the chief god in charge of all the money issues and prosperity in Heaven and Earth.

Other deities belonging to Zhao Gongming's "treasury bureaucracy" include Fan Li, a fair-skinned and suave minister from the Spring and Autumn Period (770–476 BC), and Guan Yu, a red-faced general during the Three Kingdom Period (220–280 AD). Fan Li is

the "Wise Cai Shen", known as a very kind, intellectual and smart fortune seeker and business operator. Many stores put up his image at the house entrance, wishing their business the same success. Guan Yu is "Warrior Cai Shen", who is famous for his integrity, loyalty and bravery. People believe Guan Yu could fight against evil and protect their property. They therefore worship him as a deity of wealth too. So do not be surprised if you see different images of the God of Wealth in different stores.

On the fifth day of the Lunar New Year, Cai Shen and his fellows are believed to descend to Earth, spreading good fortune. You may find that on the dawn of that day, Chinese love to set off an extraordinarily amount of crackers and skyrockets to warmly celebrate Cai Shen's coming. Cai Shen can be basically regarded as a positive version of Mammon or, to some extent, the Chinese Santa Claus, delivering prosperity to people who believe in him and pray for his blessings.

Right: A Cai Shen statuette
Below: Hong Bao, red packets used to hold monetary gifts

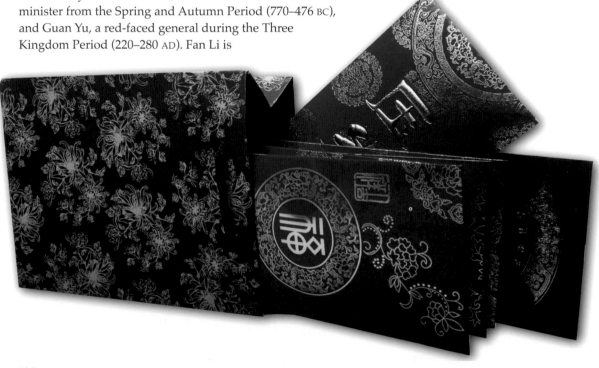

福、禄、寿、喜 FU, LU, SHOU AND XI

IN CHINESE TRADITIONAL CULTURE, Fu, Lu, Shou and Xi are the most important constituents of a quality life, denoting, respectively, good fortune, prosperity, longevity and happiness. The characters often appear on New Year's greeting cards and birthday cards. Simple and universal as they appear, they actually have profound cultural associations.

The first three, Fu, Lu and Shou, were originally associated with Taoism and can be traced back to the Ming Dynasty (1368–1644). They are each represented by a god and a heavenly star. The Fu star refers to the planet Jupiter, which is believed to bring good fortune. The God of Fu is often depicted holding a piece of calligraphy with the Chinese character "Fu". It is customary to post his picture on the front door, or simply the character "Fu", especially during Chinese New Year. The character is posted upside down because, in Chinese, "upside down" shares the same pronunciation as "arrive", and thus the upside-down post also denotes the arrival of good fortune.

Like Fu, Lu is represented by a god and a star. "Lu" literally refers to the salary of a government official, and more symbolically stands for status and wealth. The God of Lu is associated with the imperial examinations and worshipped by candidates who aspire to pass the test and rise to high office. In some places, temples are built especially for him. In traditional Chinese theatre, the God of Lu is often dressed as an imperial minister, but more often than not, he appears in paintings and drawings riding a deer, because "deer" shares the same pronunciation as "Lu".

The Shou star is the star of the South Pole in Chinese astrology, believed to control the life spans of mortals. The God of Shou appears as an old man with an extraordinarily wide and high forehead. His forehead is so featured because it bears close resemblance to that of a crane, a bird believed to have a very long life. The God of Shou also carries a walking stick. During the Han Dynasty (206 BC–220 AD), everyone over seventy years old was invited by the emperor to the palace as an honoured guest, and given a walking stick as a gift. In ancient times, the walking stick was thus not only a tool, but instilled veneration for the person holding it.

In contrast to the others, there is no god or star for Xi, but it is the most widely found of all. Xi has a variety of forms. In ancient China, it was written in a way that combined the characters of "drum" and "mouth" — beating the drums and laughing are undoubtedly signs of happiness. Today, married couples post characters of "Xi" on the front door and windows of their houses. This "Xi" is a combination of two standard Xi characters, a double form mirroring the pairing and "double joy" of marriage. Words and idioms with the character Xi carry special meanings associated with matrimony. "Xishi" (literally, "joyous event"), for instance, often denotes a wedding. "Xijiu" ("wine of joy") and "Xitang" ("candy of joy") refer respectively to the wine and candies prepared to treat guests on the occasion of a weddings. "Youxi" ("to have happiness") denotes the coming of a child — that the couple has succeeded in creating a new life.

伏羲和女娲 FUXI AND NÜWA

IN CHINESE MYTHOLOGY, Fuxi and Nüwa are the progenitors of man, originally a pair of siblings. Nüwa is best known as the female saviour of the world who mended a riven sky, while Fuxi, associated with hunting, divination and music, embodies a civilizing force. Worshipped as gods in the ancient world, Fuxi and Nüwa are often depicted as figures with human heads and snake or loong bodies, with their tails entangled.

According to myth, many aeons ago the sky had collapsed when the angry god Gonggong crashed into one of the mountains that acted as its supporting pillars. Holes appeared in the sky, and a savage flood rushed forth from the heavens, carrying away all living things. Responding to the calamity, Nüwa melted stones of five different colours and used them to fill the holes, thus mending the broken sky.

When the sky was made whole again and the flooding ceased, Nüwa found the world an empty, lifeless place. She thus decided to create human beings. She moulded figures from clay and then brought them to life. Later, when she grew weary, she simply dipped a piece of rope into the wet clay and, abruptly lifting it up, dropped small lumps of clay onto the ground. Each lump became a person. In the end, Nüwa was too exhausted to continue even this, so she asked the humans she had created to produce children themselves.

While Nüwa was busily engaged in creating humans, Fuxi taught them how to fish, write and play music. It is said that he invented the qin (a Chinese zither) and introduced music to man. Studying the laws of nature, Fuxi discovered that everything arose from the interplay of yin and yang, two fundamental forces of the universe. To teach this, he devised the Eight Diagrams, with the help of which man could discern the world around him and observe the forces at play — what we would later understand as divination.

Fuxi and Nüwa

195

观音 GUANYIN

GUANYIN, or Avalokiteshvara, is the Bodhisattva of Compassion, one of the most popular figures in Mahayana Buddhism. In Chinese culture, she is depicted as a graceful woman sitting or standing above a lotus. Guanyin (literally, "observing the sounds of the world") embodies one who is sympathetic to the suffering of one and all, who answers all calls of help when her name is uttered in sincerity.

Of unimaginable wisdom and encompassing mercy, Guanyin can take various forms of incarnation — man or woman, young or old, rich or poor, king or beggar — so as to help people out of trouble, depending on their individual needs. In the many statues and images of Guanyin throughout East Asia, she is sometimes depicted with myriad arms and eyes as a testimony to her omniscience and omnipotence.

The popular 1980s TV series *Journey to the West* popularized Guanyin as the saviour of the pilgrims on their journey to the Buddhist holy land of India. The pilgrims faced many tribulations on their way, some of which seemed insurmountable even for the Monkey King. In most cases it was Guanyin who came to the rescue, descending to the earth and overpowering the monsters.

Guanyin has acquired a large following not only among Buddhists but among the larger populace. She is worshipped for her kind-heartedness and readiness to help all people. Some scholars have even attempted to draw similarities between Guanyin and the Virgin Mary of Christianity.

济公 JI GONG

THE ECCENTRIC JI GONG, allegedly a living Buddha of the Southern Song Dynasty (1127–1279), is one of best-loved characters of Chinese history. According to legend, he was a child prodigy who became enlightened and wandered around eastern China, helping the poor and punishing the corrupt with his magical powers. While being a monk, he championed a liberated lifestyle, refusing to be vegetarian and enjoying all kinds of wines and meat. At the same time, he performed miracles to cure people of diseases and other ills, and punished black-hearted landlords and corrupt officials.

In history, there indeed seemed to be a monk who resembled this figure of the legends. The historical Ji Gong had no magical powers, but he was a well-learned man whose poems and writings reveal great literary prowess. He refused to work solely for the privileged ruling class, but enjoyed helping the poor with his extraordinary medical abilities. Though he was rebuked by fellow monks for his non-standard way of life, he loved his temple, and helped to collect funds for its reconstruction after it burned down during a fire.

Ji Gong came back to life in a hugely popular 1988 TV series, in which he was portrayed wearing tattered robes, carrying a broken fan and singing, "With rugged shoes and hat, I will be there whenever there is something unfair…" Travelling around, he enjoyed tricking the vicious landlords and making them pay for their exploitation of the poor farmers. Whenever people approached him for help, he punished the bad in a memorable way — such as leaving tumours on their foreheads. People worshipped him and tried to give him gifts, but he never took a penny; he simply vanished after justice was served.

嫦娥 LADY CHANG'E

CHANG'E is the Moon Goddess of Immortality in Chinese folklore. There are at least four different versions of the legend about Chang'E, in which the heroine is depicted as somewhat different figures, ranging from a charming and considerate wife to a beautiful but selfish woman. Nonetheless, all the four versions involve four essential elements: Houyi, the sun, the elixir and the moon. What follows is the most widespread version of the legend.

Houyi and Chang'E were originally immortals in the Celestial Palace who enjoyed each other's company very much. One day, ten suns appeared in the sky, causing the earth to scorch, and fierce beasts began to eat men on the earth. The Jade Emperor of Heaven, the god who ruled over heaven, asked Houyi, a superb archer, to tackle the situation and bring relief to the suffering humanity. Together with Chang'E, Houyi descended from the heaven onto the earth and, with his superb skills in archery, killed numerous beasts and monsters. He also shot down nine suns and left only one to light and heat the earth. People on the earth were overjoyed at this and praised Houyi highly for what he did for them. The Jade Emperor, however, became furious because the suns Houyi shot down were actually His Majesty's sons. As a punishment, he turned Houyi and Chang'E into mortal human beings.

Once the most beautiful goddess in heaven but now no more than a huntsman's wife who had to worry about how the next meal could be prepared, Chang'E felt herself wronged. She often blamed her husband for offending the Jade Emperor and causing her to be downgraded to a mortal woman. To beg Chang'E's pardon for all the pain he had caused her, Houyi went on an expedition to search for the elixir, which could make people live forever. Eventually he found the Queen Mother of the West, who granted him a pill of elixir and told him that only half of the pill sufficed to make a human being immortal. Happily, Houyi took the elixir home and entrusted Chang'E with its safe keeping, telling her that on the night when the moon became full they would share it so that they would become immortals on the earth.

Quite out of Houyi's expectation, Chang'E was not content with the idea of becoming a mere immortal human being; rather, she longed for her life back in heaven. So, when Houyi went out hunting, she took out the pill of elixir and swallowed the entire piece. Soon after that, she felt herself being lifted off the ground and floating towards heaven. The gods in heaven, however, were not pleased with Chang'E's selfishness. So Chang'E was not allowed to ascend to the Celestial Palace which she and Houyi used to inhabit; rather, she could only stay by herself on the moon.

Although she became a goddess again, Chang'E felt very lonely in the Moon Palace, her lunar residence, for she had no companions other than a rabbit (known as the Jade Rabbit) and a woodcutter, Wu Gang, who had tried to steal the elixir and was condemned by gods to cut a tree that could never fall. In her lonely life on the moon, Chang'E came to regret that she had not shared the elixir with her husband. So she pleaded with the Queen Mother of the West

At 6:05am on October 24, 2007, Chang'E No.1, the first Chinese moon probe, was launched successfully from the launch centre in Jiuquan

to give Houyi another pill of elixir. Houyi did get the pill, but was only allowed to ascend to the sun instead of the moon, and the couple could not meet each other except on the 15th day of the eighth lunar month each year. On the night of that day, people in China would set an altar in their yards to offer moon cakes and other delicacies to their Moon Goddess of Immortality. Family members, lovers, and friends would share moon cakes among themselves to celebrate the reunion of Chang'E and Houyi on the full and bright moon. It was from that tradition that the Mid-Autumn Festival, a major Chinese holiday related especially to family reunion, came into being.

梁山伯与祝英台 LIANG SHANBO AND ZHU YIZNGTAI (BUTTERFLY LOVERS)

THE ROMANCE OF Liang Shanbo and Zhu Yingtai, also known as the Butterfly Lovers, is one of the best-known love stories in China. A tragic tale of yearning and loss, it tells of a couple separated by the orders of her family and reunited in death, just like *Romeo and Juliet*. Admiring the couple's chastity and devotion to each other, people speak fondly of their story to this day. Seeing a pair of butterflies, they would sometimes whisper to each other, "Don't disturb them. They are Liang Shanbo and Zhu Yingtai."

The tale is based on the real-life story of a young man named Liang Shanbo and a girl named Zhu Yingtai, with the earliest records dating from the early Tang Dynasty (618–907). As the story goes, Zhu Yingtai had disguised herself as a man and travelled away from home to pursue her studies, a rare act for a young woman at the time. For three years, she studied under the same roof as the talented scholar Liang Shanbo. While they harboured an intimate friendship, however, Zhu never revealed her true identity as a woman, a testament to her chastity. Upon parting, she implied to Liang that a young woman in her household waited for his hand in marriage, if he so desired.

Liang promised to visit Zhu once he had completed the imperial examinations. Several months later, when he came to fulfill his promise, he discovered that the young woman was Zhu herself. He immediately sought her hand in marriage. During his absence, however, Zhu had become engaged to another man, named Ma Wencai, on her father's orders.

In faithfulness to Zhu, Liang vowed never to marry, and for the next three years he served as governor of a small county. He was eventually overcome by grief and died in great sadness, buried in the vicinity of Zhu's village, unknown to Zhu. On the day of Zhu's marriage, en route to the home of the groom, the wedding procession was interrupted by a violent storm. The bride gazed out of her bridal sedan chair and saw a tomb by the wayside, and inquiring, she discovered that Liang had passed away and that it was his tomb. As she dashed out in grief, the ground suddenly opened beneath her. She leapt into the tomb, thus joining Liang in death. According to lore, from the tomb two butterflies fluttered forth, possessing a strange beauty.

木兰 MULAN

IN CHINA'S long history, dominated by figures of great male warriors, Mulan stands out as an exceptional heroine — a female warrior who, disguised as a man, takes the place of her elderly father on the battlefield when he was drafted into the army. After years of war, and crowned with accolades upon her victorious return, Mulan elects to return home to her father and her boudoir, and only then is her female identity revealed. While we know little about the historical figure of Mulan, or whether her myths were indeed based on a real-life figure, what we do know comes primarily from a stirring folk ballad, *The Ballad of Mulan*, dating from the 6th century.

The ballad begins with the sound of the loom, where Mulan was weaving and pondering over the news of the draft. The borders were encroached by warring nomadic tribes and the country was gearing up for war. The draft demanded every family to send a man, yet Mulan's father was elderly and he had no son old enough. In place of her father, Mulan stepped forward, securing for herself a horse and saddle and adopting the guise of a soldier.

Mulan spent the next ten years on the battlefield, where many perished and where she fought with exceptional valour. After ten years of unceasing conflict, the warring tribes surrendered and Mulan returned with her comrades to the palace, where they were warmly received by the emperor as great heroes. When the emperor asked Mulan what she desired, Mulan declined power and high office and asked only to go back home.

Hearing of her return, Mulan's now ageing parents staggered to greet her, and her siblings prepared a grand feast. Mulan went into to her former room, taking off her uniform and slipping into her dress, arranging her hair and ornaments before the mirror. When she emerged as woman before her comrades, they were shocked to discover that for the last decade they had fought alongside a woman. The ballad ends with a metaphor: "When two hares run side by side, who can tell if one of them is female?"

Mulan became a successful animated movie from Disney

孙悟空 THE MONKEY KING

SUN WUKONG, popularly known as the Monkey King, is a heroic character in the 16th-century Chinese novel *Journey to the West*. Embodying both the human and the supernatural, Sun has become an endearing cultural symbol among young and old alike, an unconventional pilgrim and champion of freedom in a world bound by the rules of both heaven and earth.

Sun is endowed with a number of supernatural abilities. He can transform himself to seventy two different forms of existence. He can step onto clouds and travel at tremendous speed. His extremely sharp eyes can see through any demons's disguise. His weapon, a cudgel stick, can become any size he wishes. And in battle, when facing a disproportionately large number of enemies, the monkey only needs to pull off some of his hairs, each of which turns into a clone of himself and fights just like him.

With his extraordinary abilities, Sun naturally did not submit easily to authority, and manifested great disobedience to the authorities of both the celestial and mortal realms. He claimed himself as "the great deity as powerful as the heavens", fought his way all across the celestial kingdom, and defeated tens of thousands of heavenly troops. Finally, the Jade Emperor of Heaven appealed to Buddha to vanquish the unruly monkey. Sun intended to beat up the Buddha as well. As it turned out, the Buddha out-magicked him and put him under a mountain where he waited for his redemption.

Five centuries later, the monkey was released from the mountain when he was chosen to escort Xuanzang, a great Chinese monk, to the Buddhist holy land of India to retrieve sutras. Disobedient as he was, throughout the journey Sun Wukong remained loyal to his master Xuanzang, who was frequently frustratingly ignorant and wrongfully compassionate (as he was a mortal after all, and could not recognize demons in disguise). Sun was dismissed a number of times by his master for his violent behaviour, but every time, the monkey would return to the rescue once he learned that his master was in peril. Together with two other disciples, Sun Wukong helped Xuanzang surmount eighty-one tribulations involving various demons and calamities. In the end, they retrieved the sutras from the holy land, and became dubbed saints in the Buddhist canon.

Sun Wukong's most memorable traits are defiance and loyalty, two seemingly contradictory parts of his personality which make him so human. There are a number of Chinese idioms and expressions involving the monkey whose origins can be traced back to the *Journey to the West*. For instance, a naughty child is described to be "as wild as the Monkey King". If a naughty boy happens to have a family name Sun, chances are that his nickname will be Monkey Sun. If a person has sharp eyes or is keen in judgment, he is said to possess Sun Wukong's eyes.

Sun Wukong is the protagonist for a number of movies, TV series and even video games. The TV series *Journey to the West*, shot by China Central Television in the 1980s, has left a lasting legacy on reinterpretations of the story. Jet Li, a world-renowned action star, portrayed the monkey in the 2008 release of *The Forbidden Kingdom*, which condensed many elements of the story into a single narrative.

The Monkey King images in various forms

钟馗 ZHONG KUI

ZHONG KUI is a mythical figure of Chinese folklore, the ghost catcher who is believed to terrify all demonic things. In the past, people often painted or pasted his image onto their front doors to exorcize evil beings.

According to legend, Zhong Kui was originally a talented scholar of the Tang Dynasty (618–907). He won first place in the imperial rexaminations which took place in the capital city of Chang'an, but because of his hideous complexion, he was denied admission to the court. In a burst of anger, the fiery-tempered Zhong Kui rammed himself against a palace pillar and dropped dead on the spot. Because he was an upright man during his lifetime, he was appointed the commander of all the ghosts in the underworld.

One night several years later, the emperor had a frightful dream in which a goblin stole a jade flute from him. Terrified, he cried for help. A brawny figure of hideous complexion appeared before him, caught the goblin, stuffed it into his mouth, and swallowed it. Then he told the still-trembling emperor that his name was Zhong Kui. As the emperor woke up, he asked the court painter to paint an image of his saviour, to be hung in the palace for his protection. Later on, ordinary people would similarly beseech Zhong Kui to protect them.

In the dramatic literature, Zhong Kui returned to the mortal world to marry his sister to his friend Du Ping, who had gone with him to the capital for the imperial examinations and eventually became a high official. After Zhong Kui's death, Du was the only person who dared to bury him, and in return for his loyalty and friendship, Zhong Kui married his sister to Du.

His images are often on the front doors

A painting of the fearsome Zhong Kui

8

FAMOUS FIGURES

人物荟萃

阿Q AH Q

AH Q IS THE FAMOUS PROTAGONIST of *The True Story of Ah Q* by Lu Xun (1881–1936), Chinese writer and master satirist of the early 20th century. At once pitiful and self-aggrandizing, fawning and bullying, Ah Q embodies the lowly individual who wallows in self-deception, the ultimate failure of character whose tragedy lies in his ignorance. Lu Xun, astute observer of his times and his people, launches in the story of Ah Q a sharp critique of the darker sides of the human character and of his Chinese contemporaries.

Ah Q is best know for his invention of mental victory — he constantly convinces himself that he is superior to his oppressors while in reality he succumbs to them. To be fair, everyone finds his or her own way to deal with his failures, perhaps with a little delusion, but Ah Q went too far. After being beaten and robbed, he slapped his own face to prove himself the winner; after being spanked by the landlord, he felt proud, for he now had some connection to the wealthy and powerful (albeit a less than desirable one by sensible standards). He ridiculed the residents in another town (in private, of course) for calling a long bench a straight bench, and decided that they were wrong and inferior. And Ah Q was mean. He harassed a young nun, someone who could not fight back, to feel he had got even after being bullied by others.

The death of Ah Q was as ludicrous — and tragic — as his life. When the revolution came to town, all the locals, including the wealthy landlords, became so-called "revolutionaries". Adopting the fashion, Ah Q claimed to be a revolutionary too. But before he could do anything truly revolutionary, he was arrested as a scapegoat for a crime and sentenced to death. The irony of his life lasted till the very end of his days. When signing the confession, he was worried that the circle he drew (as a substitute for his name, for he was illiterate) was not a perfect circle.

Absurd as Ah Q's life was, every reader — and every person who has a weakness — can find a familiar trace in Ah Q. The influence of his story on Chinese culture is profound. To this day, people will mock someone as "Ah Q" if he tries to round out his defeat with excuses.

包拯 BAO ZHENG

PERHAPS THE BEST-KNOWN magistrate in Chinese history, Bao Zheng is a figure of righteousness and wisdom, emboldened in the dramatic literature and popular culture to mythic proportions. Also known as "Lord Bao" (Bao Gong) and "Clear-Blue-Sky Bao" (Bao Qingtian), he is at once a saviour and a grim arbiter, who brings justice under heaven to all who cross his path.

The real-life figure of Bao Zheng (999–1062) was an official of the Northern Song Dyasty, born in Hefei (in present-day Anhui Province). He passed the imperial examinations at the age of 29, and subsequently was appointed to the court, but deferred his appointment to return to his village to serve his ageing parents, and was lauded in historical records for this act of filial piety. He returned to office years later, first as the governor of Tianchang Prefecture (in present-day Anhui Province) and later as emissary to the border Khitan region. He served in various noted posts, including as the mayor of the then-capital city of Kaifeng.

It is said that Bao Zheng was an austere man with a dark complexion who rarely smiled. Firm and righteous, he battled against corruption in court, and was beloved and esteemed by the poor and the exploited. According to legend, he possessed three sets of guillotines: one used for executing ordinary criminals; one for court officials; and the last for the violators from the imperial family. He is also said to have possessed a sword from the emperor, which authorized him to execute any man on the spot, including those in positions of power. As the story goes, Bao Zheng once executed a powerful eunuch who abandoned a newborn prince, and at another time sentenced the emperor's son-in-law to death for attempting to murder his wife and children from a previous marriage.

In the 1990s, various TV series revived popular interest in Bao Zheng, who remains a well-loved figure today. Paying homage to him, people visit his grave in his hometown of Hefei, where a temple has been erected to commemorate his righteous life.

The statue of Bao Zheng in the temple at Hefei

Bao Zheng (black-faced) portrayed in an opera

孔子 CONFUCIUS

BORN IN QUFU, Shandong Province, Confucius (551–479 BC) was the pre-eminent Chinese thinker, educator, and social philosopher whose teachings and philosophy have deeply influenced the whole world — but particularly eastern countries such as China, Korea, Japan and Vietnam.

Confucianism is the most famous philosophical school in the history of China; it emphasizes personal and governmental morality, and proper social relationships, justice and sincerity. At the centre of Confucius' thought is Ren (goodness or benevolence) and its form of expression is Li (the Rites). These values gained prominence in China over rival doctrines such as Legalism or Taoism during the Han Dynasty (206 BC–220 AD). Now known as Confucianism, this philosophy was introduced to the West by the Jesuit priest Matteo Ricci.

Famous in his own lifetime, Confucius travelled from state to state preaching his doctrines, but in his last years he stayed at home compiling and editing books. His most important sayings were recorded in *Lun Yu* (*Analects of Confucius*), a collection of "brief aphoristic fragments" which were compiled by his disciples after his death.

Confucius failed to realize his political ideals during his lifetime, but after his death his philosophy has continued to influence Chinese thought for over 2,500 years. His doctrines on morality and ethics have had a great effect on Chinese ideology.

孔廟曲阜 TEMPLE AND CEMETERY OF CONFUCIUS AND THE KONG FAMILY MANSION, QUFU

THE CITY OF QUFU, in Shandong Province, is said to be the birthplace of the notable Chinese scholar and philosopher Kongzi, commonly known as Confucius (551–479 BC). The capital city of the State of Lu during the Spring and Autumn period (770–476 BC), Qufu is today known for its significant architectural collection associated with Confucius and his descendants. This includes the Cemetery of Confucius, the Kong Family Mansion and the Confucius Temple, presently the second-largest historical building complex in China after the Forbidden City.

A year after Confucius died, the King of Lu ordered his former residence to be consecrated as a temple. This event marked the canonization of Confucianism by the Chinese feudal authorities. In 195 BC Liu Bang (reigned 206–195 BC), the first emperor of the Han Dynasty (202 BC–220 AD), offered sacrifice to Confucius in Qufu. Liu set an example for succeeding emperors, who would visit the temple on important occasions. In total, more than one hundred emperors visited or sent their representatives to Qufu to pay homage to Confucius.

Throughout history, the Temple complex has undergone no less than fifteen renovations, with a major expansion during the Song Dynasty (960–1279). The present complex encompasses a total of 466 rooms with beautiful yellow roof-tiles and red walls, with their style and layout resembling that of the imperial palace. The main part of the complex, oriented north-south, consists of nine courtyards lying on a central axis. Within its outer wall, with four corner towers, are numerous ancient pine trees. The temple complex is also home to some 2,000 ancient steles and many richly decorated pillars.

To the north of Qufu lies the Cemetery of Confucius, where the family and descendants of Confucius are buried. With more than a thousand tombs, the cemetery records a geneology of 2,340 years, across the longest line of descendants in the world. The most recent tombs belong to descendants of the Kong family of the 76th and 78th generations. As the family was conferred the status of nobility, and many of its descendants wedded princesses of the imperial court, status symbols of noblemen can frequently be found among the tombs.

The Kong family mansion, where the descendants of Confucius lived, is located to the east of the Temple. Its residents were in charge of tending to the Temple and the Cemetery, and were responsible for conducting various ritual ceremonies on occasions such as plantings and harvests. In a sense, Confucius' descendants were in charge of the largest private estate in China. The layout of the mansion is traditional, with residences in the rear, and the buildings placed in hierarchy, reflecting Confucian principles of order and patriarchy. With more than 400 rooms, the mansion is replete with exquisite furnishings, decorations and relics, including gifts from emperors and high-ranking officials.

四大美女 THE FOUR BEAUTIES

ACCORDING TO LEGEND, the Four Beauties were the most beautiful women of ancient China, three of whom brought kingdoms to their knees. They lived during different dynasties, each hundreds of years apart. In order, they were Xi Shi (who lived during 700–600 BC, or around the time of the Spring and Autumn period), Wang Zhaojun (who lived during the 1st century BC, or the Western Han Dynasty), Diaochan (who lived during the 3rd century AD, or the Three Kingdoms period), and Yang Yuhuan (719–756, of the Tang Dynasty).

LIVES

XI SHI was born in a village in present-day Zhejiang Province, a woman of the State of Yue. Renowned for her beauty, she was given to Fuchai, king of the Wu State, as a gift from Goujian, king of the Yue State. Using her wisdom, Xi Shi enchanted Fuchai and became his most beloved consort. While Fuchai lavished his attention upon her, he neglected the affairs of his kingdom. This gave the Yue State ample time to prepare for its attack on the Wu State, which ultimately resulted in the annihilation of the latter.

Above: Shadow puppets of Wang Zhaojun

Five centuries after Xi Shi, Wang Zhaojun appeared, another important woman in Chinese history. Chosen as an imperial concubine for her beauty and intelligence, she was nevertheless unknown to the emperor for years. When the leader of the northern Xiongnu tribes, then viewed as barbarians, negotiated peace with the emperor and proposed a political marriage, she volunteered to go with him, and her beauty astounded the court. Another version of the story has it that Zhaojun offended court officials with her proud temperament, which resulted in her designation as a political bride and peace offering. Nevertheless, she is credited with enabling peace between the Han imperial court and the Xiongnu tribes for over 50 years.

Diaochan, unlike the other three, has no historical account relating her to a real-life figure. She appears in *the Romance of the Three Kingdoms*, where she is described as having been involved in an affair with two men. She brought about jealousy between the warrior Lü Bu and his godfather, the treacherous court official Dong Zhuo, both her lovers, which ultimately resulted in Lü killing Dong. In the novel, she appears a courageous and beautiful woman in a world dominated by men. In the official history of the Han Dynasty, however, only Dong Zhuo's servant girl is mentioned, and no clear evidence links her to the Diaochan of the novel.

The last of the four beauties, Yang Yuhuan, was the beloved concubine of Emperor Xuanzong of the Tang Dynasty. When the two first met, Yang was 22 and the emperor was 56 years old. Infatuated with her, he employed over 700 tailors in her service, and knowing lychees were her favourite fruit, ordered them to be transported over thousands of miles to the capital each year. She captured his attention so much that many attributed the decline of the Tang Dynasty to her; indulging in his love for her, Xuanzong neglected state affairs in his later years, while corrupt officials dominated the court and border skirmishes threatened the peace of the land. The famed play *Palace of Eternal Life* dramatizes their decadent romance and its tragic ending, as the emperor gave up Yang to be hanged when his men threatened to mutiny on their escape from a sudden rebellion.

ANECDOTES

Throughout the centuries, poets and painters were enchanted by the four beauties, and lavished praise on their radiance. Xi Shi is said to have been so beautiful that, when she walked by water, the fish would forget to swim and sink away from the surface. Wang Zhaojun's beauty attracted birds in flight to fall from the sky. Diaochan was so radiant that the moon shied away in embarrassment. Yang Yuhuan's complexion was such that the sight of her face put all flowers to shame. When she walked around the garden and touched the flowers, the petals would close in shyness.

Despite their beauty, what makes the four women memorable is their quirks. Xi Shi is said to have had feet larger than those of any Chinese women of her time. She also suffered from constant chest pain, and when she winced in pain she blushed, making her appear lovelier than ever. As for Wang Zhaojun, she is said to have had uneven shoulders. Diaochan had one eye bigger than the other. Yang Yuhuan suffered from body malodour, which she attempted to wash away with lavish baths and to cover up with scented powder. She was also rather plump by today's standards.

成吉思汗 GENGHIS KHAN

TEMÜJIN, more often known by his title Genghis Khan, is regarded as the first emperor of the Yuan Dynasty (1206–1368), though it was his grandson, Kublai Khan, who elevated him to this position posthumously. Genghis Khan unified the Mongol tribes and established a great empire, which was further expanded by his successors into probably the largest empire the world has ever known. His achievements made him one of the greatest military commanders and statesmen in history.

He was born in 1162 and endured a difficult childhood, particularly after his father's death. He survived with help from friends and allies who would become his main advisors and generals in the future. The first step in his rise to power was within his own people — in 1189, Temüjin became leader of his own tribe. Next he united the many other Mongol tribes, who were entangled in complicated alliances and tribal confederations that led to regular warfare. The main tribes were the Keraits, Merkits, Naimans, Tatars and Uyghars; the last to fall to him were the Naimans, defeated by his greatest general, Subutai. After this he was acknowledged as the Khan of the whole of Mongolia in 1206, and was honoured as Genghis Khan (Genghis means "sea" or "strong" in the Mongol language).

Control of the Mongol tribes was just the beginning of Genghis Khan's glorious but cruel reign. His well-armed and well-led troops proved unstoppable, and for the next 20 years his empire was expanded by many military campaigns. From 1205 to 1209, he raided the Western Xia Empire three times, causing great damage, and forcing it to sue for peace. From 1211 to 1215, he attacked the Jin Empire twice, taking its northern territories: its capital (today's Beijing) fell in 1215.

Above and Below: The Mausoleum of Genghis Khan, Xinjie Town, Inner Mongolia, China

In 1218, he destroyed the Western Liao Empire (also known as the Khara-Kitan Khanate) before moving further west in 1219. He first crushed the Khwarezmid Empire, and then his armies crossed the southern Caucasus Mountains and reached southern Russia. After defeating the Russian princes in 1223 — and learning about the abundant lands beyond that would lead to further western adventures by his successors — he returned east in 1226, to punish the Western Xia and Jin Empires for rising against him. He died of illness in 1227 just before their surrender. He was buried in great secrecy in a hidden grave that has yet to be discovered. His successors would continue fighting and established the Yuan Dynasty in 1271.

Genghis Khan built a military state but it is wrong to think of him as simply a destroyer. His simple but effective system of government and laws put an end to the continuous wars among the Mongol tribes, allowing them to prosper. They began to use a written language, which was based on the alphabet borrowed from the Weiwuer people. He is venerated today both in Mongolia and China.

关公 GUAN YU

The character Guan Gong regularly appears in the Peking Opera

GUAN YU (also known as Guan Gong—"Sir Guan") was a legendary warrior and general who lived during the Three Kingdoms period (220–280). Allegedly over 6ft 6in (2m) tall, he is known as the Martial King, and appears in dramatic literature as a giant with almond-shaped eyes and a long beard, wearing a green warrior costume and carrying a long-handled scimitar. In *The Romance of the Three Kingdoms*, Guan appears as a fierce warrior, who charged straight into the enemies' lands and killed the rival generals amidst thousands of enemy troops. Guan's image is found not only in literature, but also appears in temples throughout China and East Asia, where he is worshipped as a god.

According to *The Romance of the Three Kingdoms*, Guan met the generals Liu Bei and Zhang Fei and swore brotherhood with them, united by a common, lofty vision to save and protect the people. Guan remained faithful to his sworn brothers until death, even when he was offered extremely appealing gifts and positions to join the enemy ranks. When he and two of Liu Bei's wives were captured by Cao Cao, Liu's archrival, he agreed to fight for Cao in order to keep Liu's wives safe. Yet, when he learned of Liu's whereabouts, he immediately took off after his sworn brother, leaving behind all the gifts Cao gave him. Escorting Liu's wives for hundreds of miles, he finally became reunited with his two sworn brothers. Cao was so moved by Guan's loyalty that he ordered his troops not to stop him.

Guan's fierce spirit as a warrior makes him a natural hero among men of arms, but he has grown to be worshipped by the general populace as well. In the Confucian canon, Guan appears as a skilled warrior who was also an honourable civil leader. Because he is said to have been in charge of commerce in Liu's kingdom, which flourished and prospered, Guan is sometimes worshipped as the god of commerce by merchants and businessmen. Among the populace, Guan appears as an all-powerful deity. People pray to him for rain, for medicine, for safety and for peace. Guan's temples are found not only in China but also in a number of Southeast Asian countries.

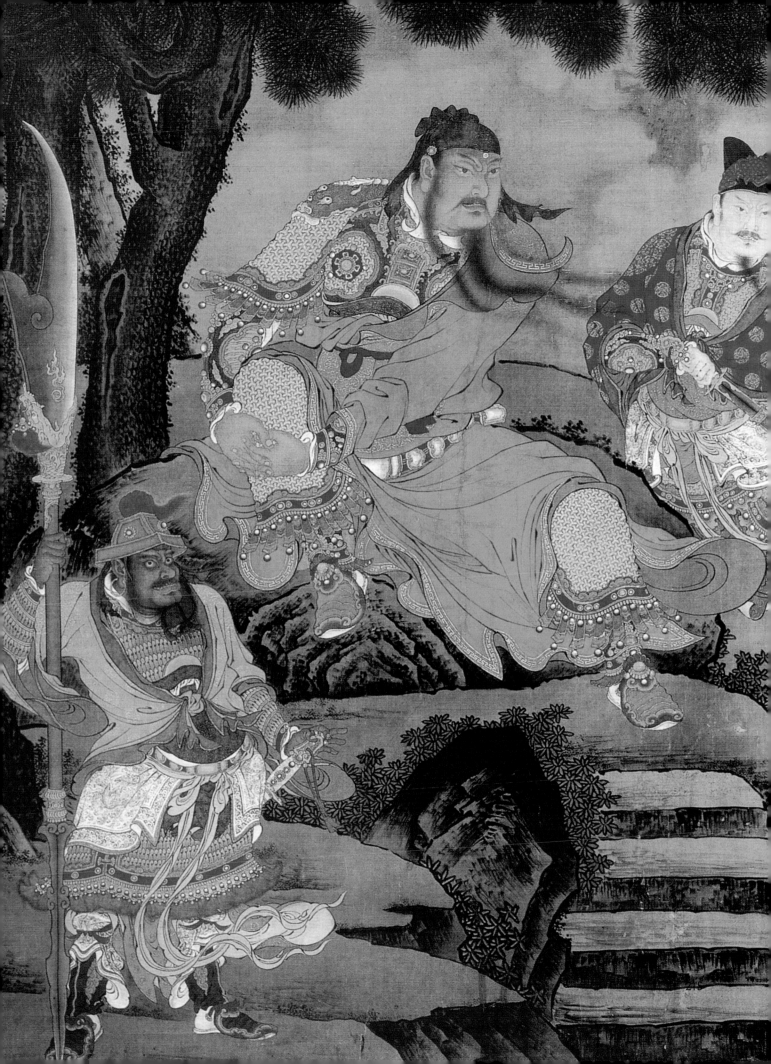

老子 LAO TZU

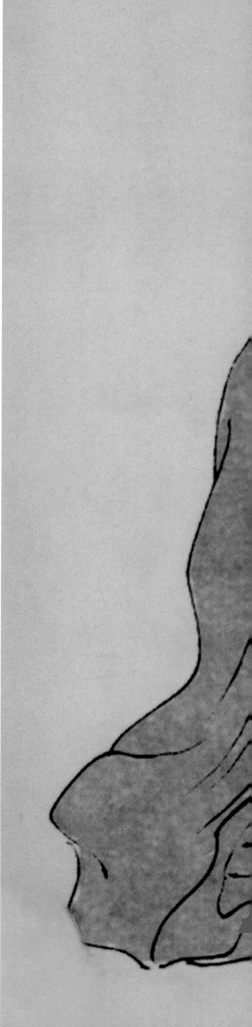

GENERALLY RECOGNIZED as the founder of the philosophy of Taoism, Lao Tzu (also spelled Laozi) occupies a very significant position in the intellectual and cultural tradition of China. *Tao Te Ching*, the principal classic of Taoism, is attributed to him.

Despite the many legends, we know little about Lao Tzu and his life. He is believed to have lived in the 6th century BC and been called Li Erh, serving as the curator of the royal library of the Zhou Dynasty; one story goes that Confucius once asked him for teachings on rituals.

Tao Te Ching (also called *Laozi*), is probably the most widely translated Chinese work of all time. This 81-chapter masterpiece is divided into two parts, *Tao Ching* and *Te Ching*, and although it only has only 5,000-odd characters, its richness cannot be overstated — it covers various fields from cosmology to morality, from political principles to religious practices. The central concept of this book is Tao, which is the mother of being and also manifests itself in the principles of the universe. Tao is omnipresent but cannot be observed by any sense — its two major characteristics are emptiness and quietness.

Another important concept of Taoism is non-action (wu wei), which means doing nothing against Tao; it is the Taoist ideal for government. According to Lao Tzu, governors should control their desires and avoid disturbing people with heavy taxes, and the ruling class should keep the virtue of quietness and thus set a good example to encourage people to live a simple and peaceful life. Additionally, when Tao is lost wisdom and morality arise as remedies. Only when society is troubled by stupidity and immorality do people expect wise and moral sages to help them out.

Tao Te Ching shows deep understanding of dialectic. It points out that opposites such as big/small, weak/strong, empty/full, difficult/easy and noble/humble are interdependent and can transform into each other. Based on this observation, Lao Tzu made many profound remarks.

Lao Tzu and Zhuang Tzu, his intellectual successor, have had a notable impact on Chinese culture, so much so that their philosophies about life and society have become an underlying element of what makes the Chinese people Chinese.

秦始皇 QIN SHI HUANG

QIN SHI HUANG was the first emperor of the mighty Qin Dynasty and is celebrated for being the chief builder of the Great Wall of China and the amazing Terracotta Army. He was born Ying Zheng in 259 BC and became the king of Qin State at the age of 13, although his mother and prime minister Lu Buwei ruled as his regents. Qin Shi Huang learned his lessons well and by 238 BC he had established absolute power over his land. China at the time was split into seven major states which had been fighting each other for precedence for over a century. Qin Shi Huang conquered them one by one until in 221 BC he could announce himself as Qin Shi Huang — Qin being the name of his state and new dynasty; shi meaning first; and huang meaning emperor.

Once in complete control of China, Qin Shi Huang changed the established order. He abolished the old feudal system and divided the country into counties, each under the direct control of the central government with himself as the sovereign authority. He also standardized the currency and built a vast network of roads and canals so that every part of China was well connected to its neighbour and beyond. Even more importantly, Qin Shi Huang ordered that the same written language should be used all over China. The historic significance of this to the growth of Chinese civilization and culture is difficult to overstate.

Throughout his reign Qin Shi Huang built projects on a monumental scale. His most famous construction was his own vast subterranean mausoleum, effectively an underground city, guarded by his remarkable terracotta army. Another gigantic project was the Great Wall of China, which he ordered built into a continuous wall from the numerous old defensive walls built by rival states. Unfortunately his other grandiose project, the E'pang Palace, said to be big enough to contain ten thousand people, was destroyed in a big fire.

Qin Shi Huang died at the age of 50 while touring eastern China. His empire collapsed within a few short years, thanks in no small part to the long-term heavy taxes and obligations that he placed on his subjects to pay for his grand building projects.

QIN SHI HUANG'S MAUSOLEUM

LOCATED AT THE FOOT of Lushan Hill in Lintong, Shanxi Province, this is the largest and most ambitious mausoleum in the world. It took 700,000 labourers 38 years to build and covered an area of 19 square miles (50sq.km). Even today most of the mausoleum remains buried and a mystery. Historical records claim that it housed great treasures and was modelled on the city plan of Xianyang, the capital of the Qin empire. It is said to have ceilings covered in pearls representing the stars and gems for the skies that watched over rivers and oceans of mercury. The terracotta army itself was discovered by accident in 1974 and many describe it as the eighth wonder of the world. The discovery stunned the world as its army of some 8,000 warriors came to light, each with its own distinctive features and facial expression. Additionally the army includes chariots, weapons, horses, musicians and entertainers.

The terra-cotta army of Qin Shi Huang

孙子 SUN TZU

SUN TZU, born in the same age as Confucius, is one of the most renowned philosophers of China and one of the most influential military strategists in world history. *The Art of War*, a bestseller today, outlines his thoughts on military strategies in great detail.

Sun Tzu was a man of the Spring and Autumn period (770–476 BC), a time when powerful warring states challenged the sovereignty of the declining Zhou Dynasty. In 512 BC, the southern Wu State was preparing to invade the Chu State, and the king of Wu sought a military strategist. Sun Tzu was recommended to the king by his minister Wuzixu. Sun Tzu was at the time an obscure figure, and it is said that the king agreed to see him only after seven consecutive recommendations by Wuzixu.

According to legend, the king of Wu, unconvinced by Sun Tzu's abilities, gave him the formidable task of turning his hundred and eighty concubines into a small army. In response to the request, Sun divided the concubines into two groups, with two as captains. When they took his commands as jest and continued with their boisterous ways, Sun ordered the execution of the two captains, following military procedure. Although the king pleaded for their lives, Sun proceeded with the execution and named two new captains. The concubines subsequently were much more disciplined, and soon mastered the basic tactics of combat. Upon inspecting this unique army, the king became greatly impressed with Sun Tzu.

Sun Tzu was named the commander-in-chief of the army and led the troops of Wu to successfully defeat the powerful neighbouring kingdom of Chu. Under his command, Wu became the most powerful kingdom in the south, and began to expand northward. It would eventually combine its forces with troops from the Lu State and defeat the Qi State.

Sun Tzu eventually lost favour with the king of Wu, who became increasingly complacent about his expanding empire. After the minister Wuzixu was libelled in court and committed suicide, Sun retired quietly to the countryside to complete his manuscripts on military philosophy. With succeeding invasions from the increasingly powerful Yue State, the Wu State eventually went into decline.

Although Sun Tzu served as the commander of Wu, his vision for unity transcended the narrow ambitions of territorial gain. He began his *the Art of War* with counsel on the motivations of war. He warned the king to be cautious of war, for its stakes are exceptionally high, and advised that war should be waged in the greater interest and not based on the personal sentiments of the king or general.

The Art of War is divided into thirteen chapters and systematically discusses military strategies and tactics in a variety of situations. Chapter nine, for example, discusses different ways to move and station the army with respect to different geographic situations. Chapter twelve illustrates how to use fire in battle and torch enemy camps and provisions.

The impact of *The Art of War* was deep and far-reaching, spreading throughout East Asia and as far as Europe. The manuscript, today translated into many languages, serves as inspiration for contemporary strategists and thinkers. The American General Norman Schwartzkopf, who became famous in the Gulf War, drew inspiration from this classic, as did British military strategist Liddell Hart. The American economist R. M. Hodgetts referenced the book in discussions of enterprise management, which similarly draws on strategy and tactics.

孙中山 SUN YAT-SEN

SUN YAT-SEN (1866–1925), also known as Sun Wen, was the founder of the Chinese Nationalist Party (or the Kuomintang [KMT]). He led the Chinese revolution that toppled the last imperial dynasty and initiated the process of building republican China. Regarded as a pioneering revolutionist, Dr. Sun is held in high esteem in both mainland China and Taiwan.

Born into a peasant family in Xiangshan, Guangdong

Right: Sun Yat-Sen, the founder of the Chinese Nationalist Party

Province on November 12, 1866, Sun received traditional Chinese education until he was 13 years old, when he left for Hawaii to join his elder brother Sun Mei, a prosperous merchant who had emigrated there as a labourer. In Hawaii, Sun Yat-sen enrolled at the Iolani School and very quickly learned to speak English. A few years later he arrived in Hong Kong, where he received his medical education and obtained a licence to practise medicine from the Hong Kong College of Medicine (now part of Hong Kong University).

Deeply influenced by the political ideas of Alexander Hamilton and Abraham Lincoln, and agonizing over his country's backwardness and his countrymen's conservative attitudes, Sun wrote a long letter to Li Hongzhang (1823–1901), then the most powerful politician in the imperial court. In his letter, Sun outlined suggestions for reform, only to be met with a cold rebuff from Li. Disillusioned with the imperial court, corrupt and effete as it was, Sun resigned from the medical profession and embarked on the path of revolution. In 1894, he founded the Revive China Society in Hawaii, which aimed to expel the Manchu rulers, establish a republic, and reform land ownership to relieve peasants of heavy taxes. In the next year he plotted an armed uprising, which failed. For the next 16 years he went into exile in Japan, the United States and Europe. During his stay in Japan, he won favour with dissident student groups and founded the United League (Tongmeng Hui), which merged the Revive China Society and three other revolutionary organizations.

In 1911, with the uprising in Wuchang, Sun Yat-sen returned to China to head the revolutionary movement against the Qing monarchy. Later in the same year, he was elected Provisional President of the newly born Republic of China (the official history of which began on January 1, 1912). The provisional government, however, was very fragile; while provinces in south China had declared independence from Manchu rule, north China maintained an ambivalent attitude. In an attempt to gain support from the north, Sun relinquished his presidency to Yuan Shikai (1859–1916), a powerful warlord

The Memorial Hall to Sun Yat-Sen in Guangzhou

who commanded a newly established, elite imperial army, in exchange for Yuan's alliance with the revolutionary cause. Yuan successfully forced Puyi (1906–1967), the last emperor of the Qing Dynasty, to abdicate. Not long after taking the oath of office as President in 1913, however, Yuan outlawed Sun Yat-sen and his followers and sought to restore monarchy in China. In the same year, Sun led a revolt against Yuan, which ended in failure, and he was forced back into exile.

In 1914, during exile in Japan, Sun married Soong Ching-ling (1893–1981), sister of Soong May-ling (1897–2003), the American-educated, would-be wife of Sun's political successor Chiang Kai-shek (1887–1975).

Sun returned to China in 1916, when Yuan died shortly after proclaiming himself emperor. Yuan's death had left the country torn by competing warlords. Keenly aware that the situation would erupt into anarchy, Sun attempted to set up a constitutional government in Guangdong in 1918, but failed. He spent the next five years giving speeches in Hong Kong and other places to disseminate his own political doctrine, notably the Three Principles of the People, and reflecting on his military failures.

In the late 1910s, Sun managed to establish a military government in Guangdong. He would receive assistance years later from the former Soviet Union to reorganize the Nationalist Party (Kuomingtang), which he had founded on the basis of the United League after the 1911 Revolution. Increasingly recognizing the importance of military power to the materialization of his blueprint for a new China, Sun instituted the Whampoa Military Academy in Guangzhou in 1924, with Chiang Kai-shek as its principal. Later in the same year, Dr. Sun launched the North Expedition against warlords in the northern provinces, with a view to ending factional strife and bringing the country back under the rule of a central government. Meanwhile, he went on delivering speeches to his people, stressing the significance of China's unification and the abolition of unequal treaties imposed on China by the Western powers. Despite his deteriorating health, Sun travelled north to negotiate with the warlords, hoping for unification. On March 25, 1925, he died of liver cancer in Beijing. Four years later, his remains were transported to Nanjing, then the capital of the Republic of China, and buried in Dr. Sun Yat-Sen's Mausoleum there.

Although Sun Yat-sen passed away more than eighty years ago, his legacy remains bold to all who care about the present and the future of the Chinese nation.

SUN YAT-SEN SUIT

THE SUN YAT-SEN SUIT, known in the West as the Mao suit, is actually named after the first president of the Republic of China, Sun Yat-sen (1866–1925). It emerged in the 1920s as a national dress for men in China, defining the image of a new era after the 1911 Revolution. Its popularity soared in the succeeding decades through the 1970s, when it became the iconic attire of Mao Zedong and other leaders of the Communist Party of China.

It is said that the suit originated when Sun Yat-sen asked a Shanghai clothier to tailor a military uniform into something that he could wear on casual occasions. What resulted was a suit that combined the formal appearance of a uniform with the economy and practicality of casual wear — the top doubled as a jacket and shirt; the pockets were made wide to accommodate writing materials; the two-piece was comfortable to wear and economical to make. Moreover, the simple cut of the new suit presented a

modern look that marked a radical departure from the one-piece, gown-like traditional Chinese changshan, which had come to symbolize the backwardness of dynastic China. In 1929, the Sun Yat-sen suit was declared the uniform of top-ranking officials of the Nationalist government.

Unlike the Western suit, the Sun Yat-sen suit features a turned-down collar, four outside pockets and five centre-front buttons, adhering to traditional Chinese aesthetics of simplicity, symmetry and solemnity.

The four pockets represent the Four Cardinal Principles in the *Book of Changes*: Propriety, Justice, Honesty and Conscience. The five centre-front buttons correspond to the five branches of government of the newly founded Republic of China (1912–1949): the executive, legislative and judicial branches; the censorate; and the branch responsible for civil service examinations. The three cuff-buttons symbolize Sun Yat-sen's Three Principles of the People: Nationalism, People's Power and People's Livelihood, which formed the basis of his political philosophy.

Sun Yat-sen showed his fondness for the suit by wearing it on various occasions. After the founding of the People's Republic of China in 1949, it became worn by almost the entire male population. Today, when popular taste has turned to Western suits, the Sun Yat-sen suit remains a choice attire on important occasions.

SUN YAT-SEN'S MAUSOLEUM IN NANJING

SUN YAT-SEN'S MAUSOLEUM in Nanjing is the final resting place of Sun Yat-sen. The mausoleum lies on the southern side of the Purple Mountain in Nanjing, covering an area of approximately 84,000 square yards (70,000sq.m). The mausoleum was designed by the architect Lü Yanzhi (1894–1929), a graduate of Cornell University, and constructed in the late 1920s.

Champion of the Chinese republican revolution, Sun Yat-sen founded the Chinese Nationalist Party (or the Kuomintang of China [KMT]) and the Republic of China. During his lifetime, he had toured the Purple Mountain and, impressed by the majestic views around it, he told his comrades that he wished to beg from his fellow countrymen "a cup of earth" from the mountains for his burial after his death.

Shortly after Sun passed away in Beijing on March 25, 1925, the Preparatory Committee for Dr. Sun Yat-sen's Funeral organized a competition to solicit design schemes for the mausoleum. Among more than forty proposals, Lü Yanzhi's design was unanimously selected. It depicted the shape of a bell, which symbolized a call to awakening and conveyed a message of "arousing the people for the construction of the republic". Lü was subsequently appointed chief architect of the mausoleum complex. Construction began in 1926 and finished in 1929. In late May 1929, Sun's coffin was transported to Nanjing from the Biyun Temple in Beijing, and on June 1st, Sun was laid to rest in the new mausoleum.

Situated on the south-facing slope of the Purple Mountain, the mausoleum complex is configured in the shape of a reclining bell, with the Crescent Terrace at the bottom of the slope as the bell's top and the dome-shaped Vault halfway up the mountain as the clapper. Between the terrace and the vault are a number of structures linked by flights of stone steps, measuring 164ft (50m) in width and 1,575ft (480m) in total length. In the order that they meet the eyes of a visitor walking up the steps, the structures comprise the Stone Memorial Archway, the Mausoleum Gateway, the Stele Pavilion and the Hall of Mourning. While the Stone Memorial Archway marks the entrance to the entire complex, the Mausoleum Gateway serves as the entrance to the mausoleum itself. Four Chinese characters, "Tian Xia Wei Gong" ("what is under Heaven is for all"), are inscribed on the Gateway, engraved in the style of Sun Yat-sen's own script. Behind the Gateway, the Stele Pavilion houses a 30 ft (9m) high stele erected by the Kuomingtang to commemorate the entombment of its founder.

Three arched doors, on each of which is inscribed one of the Three Principles of the People (Nationalism, People's Rights and People's Livelihood), open into the spacious marble Hall of Mourning. In the centre of the Hall sits a 15ft (4.6m) high statue of Sun Yat-sen. Carved out of Italian white marble, the statue is a famous French sculptor's masterpiece. The walls of the hall are inscribed with the complete script of *General Schemes for the Construction of China*, which Dr. Sun completed in the years from 1917 to 1920.

Two small doors on the north wall of the Hall of Mourning lead into the dome-shaped vault, which has a diameter of 60ft (18m) and a height of 36ft (11m). The centre of the vault is below ground level, housing a white marble sarcophagus on which lies a recumbent white marble statue of Dr. Sun Yat-sen. The copper coffin encasing the remains of Dr. Sun is positioned beneath the white marble coffin.

Incorporating both traditional Chinese and Western architectural elements, Dr. Sun Yat-sen's Mausoleum is viewed as the best of its kind in modern Chinese architectural history. Every year, numerous visitors from different parts of China make their way up the Purple Mountain to pay homage to Dr. Sun Yat-sen (in May 2008, for instance, Wu Po-hsiung became the first incumbent Kuomintang chairman to visit the Mausoleum since 1949). In the past eight decades, this great pioneering revolutionist has been lying quietly in this magnificent structure, commanding a view of the vast expanse of dark-green woods on the eastern outskirts of Nanjing.

Dr. Sun Yat-Sen's Mausoleum in Nanjing

炎帝和黄帝 YAN-DI AND HUANG-DI

YAN-DI AND HUANG-DI were two powerful tribal leaders active along the banks of the Yellow River around 2400 BC. They are known as the mythical ancestors of Chinese civilization; Chinese people often refer to themselves as "descendants of Yan and Huang". According to Chinese mythology, Huang-di (Emperor Huang, the Yellow Emperor) invented the Chinese calendar, weaponry and musical instruments such as the flute and the stringed guqin. His wife is said to have been the first to weave silk from silkworms, and his official Cangjie is credited with the creation of the first Chinese characters. Huang is also associated with the important text on Chinese medicine entitled *The Yellow Emperor's Classic of Internal Medicine*, and is said to have lived for one hundred years.

Like Huang, Yan-di (Emperor Yan) was a powerful tribal leader. His tribe fled to northern China when he was defeated by another tribe under the leadership of Chiyou. Competing for resources on the same land, the tribes of Huang and Yan waged war repeatedly against each other, bearing as their totems the bear and the bull respectively. Eventually, Yan's tribe merged with Huang's tribe when the latter emerged victorious, forming a powerful alliance. Yan's old foe, Chiyou, later arrived in northern China — a mythical half-man, half-beast capable of conjuring fogs and raging storms, who was eventually defeated by Huang and banished from the land. After the victory, all the tribes in northeastern China were united under the leadership of Huang, whose territory gradually expanded to the south. Different ethnic groups such as the Li, Yi, and Miao, all became integrated into the mix, reflecting the multiethnic origins of Chinese civilization.

The Mausoleum of Emperor Huang at Huangling in Shanxi Province

尧舜禹 YAO, SHUN AND YU

IN CHINESE MYTHOLOGY, Yao, Shun and Yu were three consecutive tribal leaders in the Yellow River basin from around 2300–2000 BC. In the Confucian canon, they are portrayed as ideal sovereigns, perfect sage-kings who ruled by moral example and with benevolence during a bygone era.

Yao is known for his benevolence and thriftiness. As the leader of all the tribes, he lived in a humble house and was always dressed in the same plain garments. He shared his food with his subjects, and was beloved by all of the tribes.

Yao passed the throne to Shun, who was then 53 years old. Shun is known for his diligence, modesty and most of all, his kindness. Raised by his step-mother, he had an unhappy childhood, and when he emerged as a young leader, his jealous step-siblings conspired to put him down. They made several attempts, and almost killed him once when they trapped him on the roof of a burning house. Yet with a benevolent heart, Shun forgave his step-siblings and did not try to exact revenge, even after he became the leader of all the tribes. Just like his predecessor, Shun lived humbly but worked industriously, and was always the first at work. Under his leadership, the tribes lived peacefully with each other for a long time.

Shun died at the age of 100 and relinquished the throne to Yu. Yu was chosen for his success in taming the floods that devastated all the tribes along the banks of the Yellow River. The task was originally assigned to Yu's father, who built dams everywhere trying to stop the raging floods, yet the dams collapsed and he was executed for his failure. Yu, drawing lessons from his

The Mausoleum of Yu at Shaoxing in Zhejiang Province

大禹陵·禹庙全景

father's failure, decided to build tunnels to guide the water to the sea instead of trying to block it. His flood-control methods worked very well. He was so single-minded and dedicated to this task that he didn't enter his home for thirteen years, even though he passed by the door three times. Yu eventually died during hunting, and was buried in the present-day Shaoxing. A number of emperors travelled there to pay tribute to him, including the first emperor of the Qin Dynasty, Qin Shi Huang.

The three leaders put in place a very important political system. Not one of them passed the throne to his son. Instead, each selected his successor based on his achievement and recognition among the tribes. Yao had nine sons, yet he passed the throne to Shun. It proved to be a very wise choice, as was Shun's choice of Yu.

诸葛亮 ZHUGE LIANG

ZHUGE LIANG (Zhuge being the family name), minister of the kingdom of Shu, was one of the greatest military strategists of all time. He lived during the time of the Three Kingdoms, around 200 AD, and assisted the general Liu Bei in his rise to power.

At a young age, Zhuge Liang was nicknamed by his friends the "sleeping dragon", whose potentials had yet to be awakened. Ordinary folks ridiculed him for marrying an ugly girl, who was in fact very intelligent and helped him greatly in his rise to prominence.

Zhuge Liang was not only smart about choosing his wife, but also had sharp eyes for selecting his boss. He declined the offers of several apparently powerful warlords and waited for a man of true potential. He found Liu Bei, who was then the leader of a small army only. Liu, too, held much respect for Zhuge, and visited Zhuge's dwelling three times before the latter agreed to be his advisor. The first visit, Zhuge desired to find out how sincere Liu Bei was. The second visit, he pretended to be taking a nap. Liu did not ask his servants to wake Zhuge; instead, he said that he would come again. When he returned the third time Zhuge was moved and presented to him in full detail his perception of contemporary politics and his plan to help Liu build a kingdom. Their friendship would last beyond Liu's death, when Zhuge did all he could to help Liu's son govern the kingdom, until his death on the battleground.

One of Zhuge Liang's most remarkable achievements was to persuade Sun Quan, the king of Wu, to ally with Liu Bei in a large-scale battle at the Red Cliff against Cao Cao, the most powerful warlord at that time. Zhuge Liang went to Wu alone to aid Sun Quan. In the famed battle of the Red Cliff, Zhuge demonstrated his outstanding military tactics by taking advantage of the wind to burn all of Cao Cao's warships. Only after this victory was Liu Bei able to atrengthen his own army and establish the kingdom of Shu eleven years later.

Years later, at the time of his death, Liu Bei entrusted his son to Zhuge Liang, and pleaded with his minister to help his son govern the country. The son grew into a decadent ruler, yet Zhuge Liang kept his word and remained a faithful tutor. Despite others' persuasion him to take over the throne, Zhuge Liang never sought power, but kept his word to his friend. In the historical novel Romance of the Three Kingdoms, Zhuge Liang is depicted as an epitome of wisdom. One of the best-told stories is "the Trick of an Empty City". As the story goes, Zhuge Liang was once in charge of defending a city against tens of thousands of enemy troops. At that moment, he had only a small guard in

Zhuge Liang

Kongming Lanterns, said to have been invented by Zhuge Liang, whose reverent term of address was Kongming

hand. With his insight about human psychology, he ordered to open the gate of the city to welcome the enemy, and he sat alone above the city tower, playing music in ease. This strange scenario perplexed the rival general, who suspected that there must be some big trick behind the open gate. It turned out that the ease of Zhuge Liang scared the enemy troops away, who did not make any attack and quickly withdrew.

9

PERFORMING ARTS

表演艺术

脸谱 CHINESE FACE-PAINTING

A UNIQUE FEATURE of Peking opera is face-painting. Face-painting is used as facial make-up and is a visual art in itself. In Peking opera performances, the painted face creates the atmosphere and reflects a deep psychological tie with the audience.

The forerunner of face-painting was probably the mask, which was said to have been popularized by Gao Su, a famous general in the 6th century. Unfortunately, he had feminine features and to frighten his enemies he wore a monstrous mask. Actors also used a mask when playing Gao Su, and gradually masks of different and complex design came into being, resulting in the face-painting of today.

In the development of Chinese opera, these masks were abandoned for face-painting, and powder and oil helped the facial images to emerge. The face-painting was adopted because it allowed a greater freedom of expression for the actor, since his own face was more plastic than a mask. Furthermore, it was difficult to distinguish a character's age, gender, and nationality, and actors therefore adopted colours and designs to help the audience make the differentiation.

The exaggeration and symbolism draw on the Chinese lifestyle. When looking at a painted face the audience reads its symbolic character, personality and destiny, preferring to interpret the face rather than explore the plot. The colours in the face are there to symbolize real life. The following is a guide to the basic colour scheme employed. Red is for a good, upright character, simple and loyal. White represents a crafty, conspiring character, less extroverted. Green suggests a ghostly quality. Gold is for a character of a higher, or god-like order.

The symbolic face will have a picture drawn on it — butterflies, fish or loongs. The design is associated with Chinese physiognomy. It exaggerates the eyes and the nose, and the colours of a person's face are thought to indicate his organic system and hence his personality.

The painted face is at the heart of Peking opera. Face-painting is an art, and each generation has passed on its talents to the next. In the past two centuries, Peking opera has emerged as a great art, with Beijing opera face-painting refined and perfected in the performance of today.

中国功夫 CHINESE KUNG FU

CHINESE KUNG FU, also known as Wushu or Chinese martial arts, is as Chinese as tea. Kung fu boasts a long and glorious history, enjoys great popularity in China and also has global appeal.

Kung fu was originally developed out of hunting, defence and fighting techniques. However, kung fu means more than just offence and defence. In the course of its development, different philosophies and ideas have been incorporated into its practice. Some schools of kung fu even found their inspiration from animal movements, as well as from legends and myths. Various schools of kung fu may differ in their origins, features, basic theories and technical characteristics. Each school offers a different approach to the common problems of health and self-cultivation and of offence and defence as well. Among the numerous varieties of Chinese kung fu, the Shaolin School, with a long history of over one thousand years, is the most influential.

In the practice of Chinese Kung Fu, masters have long given martial morality the highest priority when judging students, and they have made it the most important part of the training of kung fu. Martial morality includes two aspects — the morality of mind and the morality of deed. The former includes will, endurance, perseverance, patience and courage, and the latter includes respect, humility, trust, righteousness and loyalty. Masters of kung fu will normally observe students to see if they meet the standards of morality of deed, and decide whether they are worthy of teaching. The morality of mind is for self-cultivation, which one requires to perfect oneself through martial arts.

The practice of Chinese kung fu emphasizes an integration of the external and the internal: external in terms of physical actions; internal in terms of mind and breath training. The fundamentals of kung fu consist of stretching, breathing, standing, stances and stepping. Kung fu often makes use of instruments, apparatus and weapons to enhance practice. Some schools of kung fu may stress the use of meditation and static exercises.

The popularity of Chinese kung fu is largely due to its role in popular culture such as novels and movies. In China, the rise of martial-arts novels has contributed greatly to the spread of Chinese kung fu. Since the 1960s Jin Yong, the most renowned martial-arts novel writer, has published 15 novels which have been translated into English, French, German and other languages, and have won worldwide acclaim.

No account of Chinese kung fu is complete without mentioning Bruce Lee. Bruce Lee and his films are widely celebrated as having generated the worldwide interest in Chinese kung fu. He set off the worldwide kung fu upsurge and was recognized by America's *Time* magazine as "Hero and idol in the 20th century". Jackie Chan and Jet Li are also popular kung fu stars.

Recently, the film *Kung Fu Panda* (2008) has bred a new enthusiasm for kung fu. Combining Chinese kung fu with the American spirit of individual success, *Kung Fu Panda* provides a perfect example of cultural interaction and makes Chinese kung fu even more popular.

京剧 PEKING OPERA (BEIJING OPERA)

PEKING OPERA, known as Pingju, has a history dating back nearly 200 years, but despite this relatively short history it has become one of the three major "Quintessences of China" (the other two are traditional Chinese medicine and Chinese painting). As a distinct type of drama, Peking opera is very popular with audiences both at home and abroad.

Pingju lays equal emphasis on songs and dances integrated with martial art skills to create a form of traditional Chinese theatre. Often using theatrical gestures, the performance has a strong sense of rhythm that requires great technique, while the spoken parts are full of melody. As a result, a unique Chinese opera combining speech, song, dance and combat gradually came into being on the stage.

A performer in a first-class troupe is chosen for his good looks, attractive face in make-up, good physical proportions, a pair of expressive eyes and a rich variety of facial expressions. All this plus stamina and determination, as he must undergo years of rigorous training, both martial and mental. "Recite to sing, and move to dance" — an opera actor must master all these skills and combine them into one subtle and balanced art form. All his movements from the simplest of walks to stylized fights are strictly choreographed to the rhythms of the percussion and other instruments.

There are around 300 regularly performed Beijing opera plays out of a selection of over 1,300 mainly historical stories. According to the distinction between male and female, young and old, beauty and ugliness, as well as good and evil, the characters of Peking opera can be classified into four major professions — sheng (male), dan (female), jing (minor male) and chou (clown or anti-protagonist). Each profession does his or her job, and each can have many subtypes. For example, sheng generally refers to the male role, and it has numerous subtypes: lao sheng is an elderly man; xiao sheng is a young man; wusheng is someone who performs martial arts a lot.

Far right: An opera theatre
Right: Martial Arts in Peking Opera

皮影戏 SHADOW PUPPET THEATRE

THE SHADOW PUPPET THEATRE is a popular Chinese folk theatre that uses silhouettes to tell stories to music and dubbing voice. While its exact period of origin remains a mystery, it flourished during the eleventh and twelfth centuries and has remained popular ever since.

The shadow puppet theatre relies on the relationship between light and shadow in performance. The audience sits in front of a large translucent screen (the size depends on the venue) through which light passes. Performers behind the screen manipulate the puppets on sticks, and moving silhouettes of the puppets appear on the screen. Before the invention of electricity, oil lamps were used to light the screen. On average, six to seven performers and a box of puppets form a troupe, which typically has a repertoire of 40 to 50 stories.

The puppet is typically made of leather and consists of eleven pieces, representing the head, the upper body, the lower body, the two legs, the two upper arms, the two lower arms and the two hands. Alternatively, the puppet can be made from paper cuts, which is less costly but more fragile. When animated, the puppets can portray nearly all kinds of people, from grouchy old men to beautiful maidens.

太极拳 TAI CHI CHUAN

TAI CHI (also written as T'ai Chi, Taiji, Tai Chi Chuan, among others) is a form of Chinese martial arts that is impressive for its fluid, graceful and well-balanced movements. It is believed that it can promote the complete harmony of body and mind. Originally from China, Tai Chi has gained enormous popularity throughout the world for its health benefits.

When you see the slow-motion routines of Tai Chi, you might wonder whether it is really some kind of martial art. Its nature is especially confusing for Westerners because it is very different from most Western types of sport, such as rugby, where the harder and quicker the better. However, this is exactly what makes Tai Chi so unique. In Tai Chi we believe that softness is stronger than hardness, moving in a curve is better than a straight line, and yielding is more efficient than confronting.

Tai Chi has its origin in Taoism. Tai Chi Chuan means "Supreme Ultimate Boxing". The concept of "Supreme Ultimate" appears in both Taoism and Confucian philosophy where it represents the fusion of yin and yang into a single ultimate. The character "chuan" refers to a school or method of boxing or combat. Therefore, it can be said that Tai Chi Chuan, as it was originally conceived, contains a sophisticated method of fighting based on the reconciliation of dynamically interacting forces.

Now there are dozens of modern styles of Tai Chi, but we can trace their development to at least one of the five traditional schools — Chen, Yang, Wu/Hao, Wu and Sun, each named after the Chinese family from which it originated. At the beginning of its development, Tai Chi was a very potent art, guarded by a few families and used for self defence.

Tai Chi has become very popular since the early 20th century. You can see people practising it in hospitals, clinics, communities and seniors' centres. The reason for this popularity lies mainly in the health benefits that Tai Chi can bring. Today, Tai Chi has been subjected to rigorous scientific studies, and researchers have found hard proof that Tai Chi can definitely promote better health. Long-term Tai Chi practice can also help improve balance control and flexibility and can reduce pain, stress and anxiety. Moreover, it can help patients recover from many diseases.

The core training of modern Tai Chi involves two primary features. The first is the solo form, or "quan" in pinyin, which is a slow sequence of movements that emphasize a straight spin, abdominal breathing and a natural range of motion. The second is pushing hands, or "tui shou" in pinyin, which is an exercise performed by two people who are trying to improve their Tai Chi skills.

If you are interested, maybe you should try it.

REFERENCE

致谢 ACKNOWLEDGEMENTS

Text Writers:

FAN Hongsheng	KE Ping	LI Dejun	SHI Xiaogang
TIAN Zhi	XIE Shanqing	YAO Yi	YU Mei
ZHANG Yi	ZHANG Ziduan		

Text Revisers:

LU Zhenzhen received her B.A. in Anthropology and East Asian Studies from Harvard University and studied classical Chinese at Nanjing University. She was formerly a resident literary translator at Jiangsu Province Kun Opera and has traveled widely in China as a writer and ethnographer. She currently lives in New York City.

Consultants:

John A. FROEBE, Jr., former U.S. Consul General in Shenyang

Professor Paul RICHARDSON, who wrote the Introduction

For Compendium:
Design and Art Direction by Richard EVANS
Proofreading/correction by Ian WOOD
Index by Emma HOWARD

Thanks to Shirley Xie for her excellent coordination of a tricky global project.

All photographs sourced in China except:
page 3: © Werner Forman/Corbis; page 10–11: © Artkey/Corbis; page 11: © Yi Lu/Corbis; page 13: © Dave Bartruff/Corbis; page 14: © Dave Bartruff/Corbis; page 15: © Keren Su/Corbis; page 17: © Dave Bartruff/Corbis; page 18: © Swim Ink/Corbis; page 248: © Carl & Ann Purcell/Corbis

索引 INDEX

A

Abacus 152

Acupuncture 66, 152, 154
'Along the River During the Qingming Festival' 170
Amazon River 96
An Lu Shan Rebellion 22, 185
Ancestral Hall 135
Anhui Province 167, 207
Annan, Kofi 82
Art of War, The 220

B

Bai 98
Bai, Li *(701–762)* 22, 82, 162, 185
Baihua, Xin 54
Baima Mountains 98
Bamboo 36, 37, 74
Bang, Liu 209
Bashu 96
Bayan Har Mountains 103
Beauties, The Four 210
Bei, Liu 214, 228
Beijing 33, 42, 43, 107, 110, 115, 126, 155, 156, 158, 170, 184, 225, 232, 238; Olympics 25, 42, 43, 48
Bell, Johann Adam Schall von *(1591–1666)* 125
Bells, Chime 174
Bian River 170
Bird Island 77
Biyun Temple 225
Bo, Li 84
Bohai Sea 103
Broken Bridge 101
Bronzes 172, 173
Bu, Lin 35
Buck, Pearl S. 189
Buddhism 15, 41, 55, 58, 63, 77, 81, 84, 86, 88, 92, 107, 121, 123, 131, 135, 138, 177, 184, 187, 196

C

Calligraphy 28
Cangjie 15, 42, 226
Carrhae 8
Cataphracts 8

Chadao 63
Chan, Jackie 233
Chang'E, Lady 140, 197, 198
Chen Dynasty 22
Cheng, Princess Wen 123
Cheng'en, Wu 25, 131
China, Republic of 25, 31, 126, 222, 225
Chinese Nationalist Party 220, 222, 225
Chiyou 226
Chongqing 96
Chopsticks 154, 155
Chrysanthemum 37, 38
Chu, Kingdom of 137, 176, 220
Chun, Gong 181
Cixiu *(also Embroidery, Chinese)* 176
Clanglang Pavilion 107
Cleopatra 55
Clerkly Script *(also Lishu)* 16, 43
Communism 12, 15, 223
Complete Harmony, Hall of *(Zhong He Dian)* 110, 112
Confucianism 9, 12, 15, 21, 35, 63, 88, 107, 135, 208, 209, 227, 243
Confucius *(551–479 BC) also Kongzi* 21, 44, 48, 88, 110, 160, 208, 209, 220
Confucius, Temple and Cemetery of 15, 209
Courtyard house *(also siheyuan)* 155, 156, 157
Crane 19, 98
Crassus, General 8
Cypress, Han Dynasty 88

D

Da Ci'en Temple 131
Da Hong Pao Tea 92
Dabin, Shi 181
Dadu River 118
Dalai Lama 123
Di, Emperor Huang 46
Diamond Sutra 88
Diaochan 21, 210, 211
Dizhi 64, 65
Dongba 122
Dongpo, Su 36
Dongzhi 70
Dove Tree *(Davidia involucrata)* 81
Dragon 11, 32, 46, 78
Dragon Boat Festival *(also Duanwu Festival)* 137, 140
'Dream of the Red Chamber, The' 175, 177, 182
Dumplings, Chinese 157
Dunhuang 121